Be Your Own Reading Specialist

A Guide for Teachers of Grades 1-3

by

Carol Einstein

Illustrations by

Hans Neukomm

MODERN LEARNING PRESS

ROSEMONT, NJ

Reading comprehension passages on pages 78-79, 125-126, and 131
reprinted from *Reading for Content*
with the permission of
Educators Publishing Service, Inc.
31 Smith Place
Cambridge, MA 02138

Reading comprehension passages on pages 132-136
reprinted from *Reading for Concepts* and *Reading about Science*
with the permission of
Phoenix Learning Resources
12 West 31st Street
New York, NY 10001

ISBN 1–56762–064–7

Be Your Own Reading Specialist:
A Guide for Teachers of Grades 1-3

Dedication

To my parents,
who gave me the drive,

and to my husband and son,
who encouraged and helped me all the way,

with thanks and love

Acknowledgments

When I think of all the professional and personal help I received while writing this book, I am truly grateful.

To the students who make my work such a joy and from whom I learn so much, and to the teachers and reading specialists who shared their ideas, thank you.

Additional special thanks to:

Joan Amron, excellent educational therapist, diagnostician, and friend, who made valuable suggestions throughout the development of this book.

Joanne Aventuro and Anne Weiner, dedicated reading teachers at St. David's School in New York City. Besides being true professionals, they are true friends. Their reading-room doors are always open, and their feedback and encouragement as I wrote this book were much appreciated.

Joan Amman, Betsy Horowitz, Marsha Kessler, Bonnie Long, Pat Rudick, Ruth Silverman, and Jane Warwick—your help and suggestions are also much appreciated.

I am extremely grateful to my husband and son, Hans and Robert Neukomm, as well as my niece, Susanna Einstein. Their encouragement and support helped me immeasurably.

I would also like to thank Robert Low, my editor. His guidance and expertise made the task of writing this book possible.

Carol Einstein
1997

CONTENTS

PREFACE

Looking back, it seems especially interesting that I came to write this book, because I had so much difficulty learning to read in school that my mother ended up teaching me to read at home.

When I was in first grade, I went to a school for "gifted" children, which was affiliated with a local college. The school taught reading using the whole-word approach, but I was unable to learn to read that way. Toward the end of first grade, my mother, who was a high school teacher, was called into school to discuss my difficulties. And, she was cautioned by the principal not to be a "typical" teacher/mother who would try to teach me at home.

Of course, my wise mother disregarded the advice and did try to teach me at home, using the phonics-based method. I still remember quite vividly the reading work we did together, and once I broke the reading code, I became an avid reader. Since then, reading has always been a great joy.

Many years later, when I was teaching second grade in an overcrowded city school, I recognized how crucial it was for children to learn to read—as well as how difficult it was for some of them—and how much I enjoyed teaching reading. So, while continuing to teach, I went to Teachers College in New York City and earned an M.A. and M.Ed. in reading. I then worked as a reading specialist at a suburban public school, as well as at an independent day school, before going into private practice as a reading specialist.

Throughout my career, I have been fortunate to be able to work with a wide range of children. Again and again, I have seen the need to teach reading using the methods described in this book, and I have seen the very special look of wonderment—even disbelief—on children's faces when they realized they could read. This special joy is the main reason I find my work so satisfying.

Of course, I also remember so clearly the sad state that many of my students were in before they succeeded in reading. At the age of six, Jimmy was so angry that he couldn't remember his letters or numbers, he banged his head against the wall in frustration. And, as soon as Sarah, a lovely eight-year old, first tried to read with me, she just put her head on the desk in complete defeat. Both these children did learn to read, and the last time I heard from them, one was embarking on a career as a journalist, and the other was preparing to be a special ed teacher.

Experiences such as these have led me to believe that all children, not only children with reading problems, can benefit from the teaching methods described in the following pages.

CHAPTER 1

The New Environment For Teaching Reading

Teaching children to read isn't as easy as it used to be, especially for today's classroom teachers. The children have changed, conditions in the classroom have changed, and other pressures on teachers have changed, as well. The combined effects of all these changes have created a need for classroom teachers to develop and use new techniques that effectively help a wide range of students become successful and enthusiastic readers.

In the past, many classroom teachers could rely on reading specialists to assist them in teaching the students who were having the most trouble learning to read. But, dramatic increases in the number of students who are having trouble with reading—combined with the financial pressures on many schools—have resulted in many reading specialists having little or no time and space to take on additional students. Too often, a reading specialist may become "booked" very early in the year and then have to say, "I'd love to fit another student in, but I just can't take on any more." In situations like this, the classroom teacher must then be prepared to provide additional instruction and support for the students who need it.

Even when a reading specialist is helping all of the students in the class who need such help, the specialist is either taking those students away from the classroom for "pull-out" sessions, or working right in the classroom at the same time as the teacher. Either way, mutual understanding and the use of compatible techniques can clearly provide important benefits for the children and the educators.

Whatever the situation, a primary-grade classroom teacher is ultimately responsible for teaching all the students in the class to read. And, now that this responsibility has grown more onerous due to the "condition of the kids" and the switch to "inclusive classrooms," classroom teachers have all the more reason to adopt the techniques reading specialists use to help children overcome problems learning to read.

In my own work as a reading specialist during the 1980's and 1990's, for example, I have worked closely and successfully with many children diagnosed as having dyslexia or other learning disabilities. More recently, I have worked with a growing number of children diagnosed as having some sort of attention deficit disorder, and with a growing number of limited-English-proficiency students from Latin America in particular. The strategies and techniques that have helped me teach these and other students can and should be used with equal success by classroom teachers, whether or not they are assisted by reading specialists.

Before exploring these strategies and techniques in more detail, let's first take a closer look at today's children and the environments in which they are living and learning. This information provides important insights into what teachers of reading need to do—and why.

Today's Classroom Environment

Many of today's classroom teachers now work with a much more diverse and problem-ridden student population than teachers did just a few decades ago. Problems now becoming commonplace used to be seen only in special classes or were not officially recognized and treated in regular classrooms. And, not only are there now more students with problems, there are also more children who have multiple problems that require more complex solutions.

For example, many children who have an attention deficit disorder also have learning disabilities. These problems may also create some emotional problems, and the children may also be coping with side-effects of a medication taken to help with the first set of problems. So, today's teacher must not just be prepared to teach a child who has dyslexia, auditory processing problems, or an attention deficit disorder, the teacher must be prepared to teach a child who has some combination of the above along with additional, related problems. And, the same teacher may also have "gray-area" students whose reading problems cannot be easily diagnosed or treated.

Meanwhile, other children may be suffering from more basic physical problems that have either gone undetected or have not been treated effectively. Children who have not had regularly scheduled eye examinations may not realize that they are having vision problems and therefore need glasses. Children who have had recurrent ear infections that were not properly treated may suffer a temporary or permanent hearing loss, which all too often results in a language development delay. Allergies may also interfere with the learning process and require the use of additional medications in the classroom.

In today's inclusive classrooms, the physical problems can be far more severe. I know of one first grader who has cerebral palsy and sits in the classroom with a full-time aide at her side. This very smart little girl is unable to speak and communicates via a computer board, while her very responsible and competent teacher must develop new strategies to teach this student—as well as all the other students in the class—how to read.

Today's classrooms are also likely to contain minority or immigrant students whose English is not fluent. In years past, many of these students would probably have spent time in English-as-a-Second-Language classes, but now there is a growing tendency to "mainstream" them immediately. Obviously, this type of "immersion" creates additional challenges for an already over-challenged classroom teacher, who must develop effective strategies that help children learn the English language at the same time they are learning to read it well, even when they are speaking and hearing another language at home.

A classroom may also contain "gifted and talented" students who need and deserve advanced reading programs of their own. In many schools, these programs were once available outside the regular classroom but no longer are, leaving the classroom teacher with the responsibility of meeting those students' needs, as well.

And, as in previous decades, today's teachers are likely to find that some of their students are "late bloomers." Many of these children are among the chronologically youngest students in the class, but others just seem to be developing more slowly and may have a family history of late development. Either way, they may not yet be ready to complete grade-level tasks successfully, and may fail and develop negative self-images when pressured to accomplish more than they are currently ready to achieve. Other students already have poor self-images and are not motivated to work, even though they are intellectually capable of handling grade-level material. They often come from home environments in which they receive negative messages and inappropriate criticism.

Then, of course, there are also likely to be some "normal" or "average" children, who can be easily overlooked when so many other children have pressing, high-profile problems. Yet, even though these mid-range children do not have official or unofficial "special needs," they still need and deserve lots of the teacher's time and attention, as well as a reading program that matches their ability levels and interests.

The reading program described in this book is designed to help a classroom teacher work with all the children described above, so they can learn to read well and enjoy the process. This program can also help the classroom teacher overcome the trends described in the following section.

Today's Home Environment

Efforts to provide effective reading instruction for today's students are further complicated by the home life of many students. For example, I have worked with several children who were not dyslexic, but whose home life was so dysfunctional that their reading skills were severely affected. While there is often little the teacher can do to change what happens outside the classroom, the teacher must still understand the effects and be prepared to overcome them.

One prominent trend is the increase in the number of families in which both parents work. This can result in both parents feeling so rushed that they don't take time to read to their children or get books for them. Of course, this also may occur in a single-parent family. And, because children in both types of families may spend their entire day in school or engaged in other activities, when they and their parents return home at the end of the day, they may all feel too tired to do anything but sit in front of a television.

In addition, these sorts of children might have been and may still be cared for by grown-ups who speak little or no English. As Priscilla Vail points out in her book, *"Words Fail Me!"*, when children are learning by listening during their preschool years, a lack of good role models can result in language problems that do not become apparent until several years later. And, even when the children being cared for are in elementary school, caregivers who have limited proficiency in English can still limit the quality and quantity of the communication and other activities that support language development.

Children of divorced parents may also have problems learning due to the distractions and stress that can result from a family break-up. Even when there is a relatively friendly joint custody arrangement, I can often tell when students have spent the previous night with the "other" parent. It's not treated as a normal school night, and then the children are over-tired and have difficulty focusing on their work the next day.

Another trend in the homes of all sorts of families is that television and video games may be the primary source of information and entertainment. In some cases, there may be few or even no books, magazines, or newspapers. Not only do children in these sorts of homes suffer from a lack of exposure to books, they also lack role models who demonstrate that reading is both important and fun.

Obviously, there are still many homes where wise parents assign a set time to read with their children, and make a habit of stopping at the library or bookstore to obtain new books for their children. Language development may also be supported through extended conversations over meals, as well as at other times.

But, homes such as these are rarer than they once were, and that poses an additional challenge to today's classroom teachers. The solution lies in introducing a variety of reading materials that match the ability levels and interests of students, as well as teaching the students the knowledge and skills they need to read well. In order to accomplish this, however, teachers must also overcome some additional pressures from inside and outside our schools.

Today's Educational Environment

In recent years, reading instruction has been made all the more difficult at many schools by soaring enrollments and tight budgets. Resulting increases in class sizes have left teachers with even less time to meet individual needs, just when the quantity and complexity of those needs have been increasing. In addition, financial constraints have limited the availability of additional support services, often including those provided by reading specialists.

The regulations and procedures for providing support services also complicate matters for today's classroom teachers. Even when a child has been "officially" diagnosed and labeled, an Individual Education Plan may require the classroom teacher to work with the child in specific ways, and may prevent the teacher from referring the child to a specialist for additional help. Meanwhile, the classroom teacher may also have a number of specialists working with other children in the room at different times during the day, or have different groups of children leaving the room at different times to work with different specialists elsewhere. All this can be very helpful in some circumstances, but still create disruptions and tensions that interfere with the learning process.

Additional pressure may come from certain parents, who become overly zealous in their attempts to obtain services for their children and continually pressure the classroom teacher to devote more time and attention to meeting their children's specific needs. There may also be counter-pressure from other parents who feel their children are being "short-changed" because of the extensive needs of a few children. And, both groups of parents may feel that any reading problems are the sole responsibility of the classroom teacher, no matter how weak a reader the child is, or how little reading is valued and demonstrated in the home.

Obviously, this can put tremendous pressure on classroom teachers, who often have not been given the training they need to work successfully with today's wide range of children, and who are therefore concerned about being judged "incompetent." There may be an innuendo that if you cannot teach everyone in your class—no matter how disabled they are—you are not a "good" teacher.

At the same time, a variety of parents have become more concerned about the way in which all the children in the class are being taught. One reason is that the ongoing political attacks on schools and educators have created the impression that America's schools are failing to teach basic skills, and that America's teachers are more concerned about fostering students' self-esteem than providing students with needed information and skills. These concerns have been compounded by the widespread debate over the use of phonics and whole language, which has now become a political issue as well as an educational issue. And, unfortunately, due to an over-reliance on basal readers and trade books—as well as the lack of a systematic approach to teaching decoding and comprehension skills—the truth is that some children are reaching the upper grades without having been taught what they needed to become competent readers.

Now What?

With all these pressures converging in our classrooms, many primary-grade teachers are being forced to become "on-the-spot" reading specialists, without having had the training they need and deserve. These teachers are now expected to teach an increasing number of children who have serious learning problems, as well as many other children who come from homes where literacy is not valued or modeled. At the same time, the availability of reading specialists and other special services may be decreasing, while the pressure to teach all of today's students effectively and in the "right" way is increasing.

That's why the approach explained in this book can be such a valuable aid. It is based on many years of successful experience working with a wide range of students who have had problems learning to read. And, it provides a comprehensive approach to literacy, in which the systematic teaching of phonics and comprehension skills is integrated with the reading of fine children's literature and other materials that are of interest to individual students.

More specifically, this book will show you how you can:

1. Accurately evaluate the individual needs of your students;

2. Respond to those needs and teach all your students effectively through a combination of individual, small-group, and whole-class activities;

3. Provide a successful, balanced program that will earn the support of administrators and parents;

4. Help to compensate for a lack of special services and support, and successfully integrate any special services or support that are available;

5. Make your classroom function more smoothly and make you feel more satisfied with the job you are doing.

Now, let's start by examining the strategies and techniques used by reading specialists, and then see how these approaches can be adopted successfully in your classroom.

CHAPTER 2

Doing What A Reading Specialist Does

Developing a better understanding of what a reading specialist does will help you adopt effective strategies and techniques in your classroom, so you can provide your full range of students with the reading instruction they need. Your knowledge of a reading specialist's strategies and techniques will also help you work more effectively with other educators and your students' parents.

The information in this chapter grew out of my training and experience—and that of other reading specialists'—teaching children to read, especially children who are having difficulty with reading. This work includes administering and interpreting a variety of educational assessments, and then using the results to help teach readiness skills, phonics, and reading comprehension. Also, because learning to read is so intricately linked with other aspects of language development, reading specialists work with students on their writing, spelling, and other language skills.

In addition, a reading specialist serves as a resource person for other educators in the school. The specialist may conduct in-school training of teachers and consult with teachers about the needs of individual students. The specialist may also lead parent workshops on reading-related matters, and confer individually with the parents of students.

The following sections of this chapter examine key aspects of a reading specialist's work in more detail, and then provide an overview of how this approach can be adapted to your classroom.

Testing & Evaluation

The first step when starting to work with a student is to evaluate the child's knowledge and approach to reading and writing, in order to determine what and how the child needs to learn. A reading specialist may use a variety of standardized tests to gather this information, or even construct her own test. Usually, the specialist also does some informal trial teaching. The data compiled from the testing and trial teaching can then be used to develop a detailed educational plan for the student.

No matter which particular tests are used, a reading specialist usually investigates a few key aspects of language development. An "auditory blending skills" test is given to see if a student can blend sounds together to form a word. Another test evaluates a student's sight vocabulary, and yet another evaluates the child's ability to decode words, based on his or her knowledge of phonics. The latter test may use either real words or nonsense words.

A set of graded passages forms the basis for an oral reading test, which evaluates how accurately and fluently the student reads. A silent reading comprehension test is used to assess the student's understanding of what is read. The specialist may also administer a short spelling test, in which the student must write down dictated words, rather than spell them aloud.

If these evaluations show that a child is having difficulty with reading, the specialist needs to estimate the child's academic potential. A quick, effective way to do this is to ask the child for the meaning of the vocabulary words on a standardized reading test. Though not a perfect measure, vocabulary is usually the best single index of school success. And, if time is available, the specialist may also administer an individualized vocabulary test. In this type of test, the specialist says a word and the student has to decide which of several pictures best defines the word. (Of course, if the child speaks another language at home or comes from a home in which there is little exposure to standard English, this is not a true indication of the child's potential.)

For students in third grade or above, an auditory listening test may be used to determine how much the child comprehends when presented with spoken information. The specialist does this by reading a series of graded paragraphs and then asking comprehension questions.

A writing sample can also be a very valuable part of the evaluation of older children. The specialist asks the student to write a paragraph about an assigned topic, and then considers such questions as:
Is the paragraph well-organized?
Is there a sequential train of thought?
How is the spelling and punctuation?
Is the vocabulary varied?

Finally, whether the student is a beginning reader or an impaired older student, the specialist gives a brief trial-teaching lesson, in an effort to determine the best way to teach this particular child. For example, if the specialist feels that the student would favor the sight method, she might try to teach the student a few sight words. Then, she evaluates how the student responds. If this method does not seem successful, she might try another approach based on phonics or "word families." A trial-teaching lesson not only provides the specialist with valuable information, it shows the student that there is an effective way in which he or she can learn to read well.

Of course, the specialist may not have time to administer all of these tests, in which case she chooses a few, relatively quick tests. I like to use an oral reading test that includes comprehension questions, as this also gives you information about the child's reading ability and comprehension level. I may also decide to give a short achievement test, during which the child is asked to read a set of graded words. This shows how the student reads words in isolation, as well as in context.

Before using any of these tests, I always take a few minutes to talk with the student. This helps to establish a rapport and also provides me with important information. After some general conversation, I explain that what we will do together will help me find the best way to help the child learn to read well. I say that our activities will show strengths and weaknesses in reading, writing, and spelling, and this will show us what kind of work we need to do. I always say that I do not expect a perfect performance (knowing that many children worry about this), and I explain that I learn a lot from mistakes, because they show what kind of help is needed. Of course, how I say all this depends on the age and maturity of the child.

I then start the evaluation by asking some informal questions. Usually, I ask first graders to tell me their address, birthday, and telephone number, as well as the days of the week and the months of the year. Then, I might ask third graders, for example, the following questions:

What was yesterday?
What should you do if you want to find the meaning of a word?
What is a telescope?

Children usually do not feel threatened by this type of questioning, so it is a positive way to begin an evaluation. The answers also give me a sense of each child's general fund of knowledge and sequencing ability.

As we proceed with the tests, I make sure to provide encouragement. When a student makes an error, I offer reassurance by saying, "It's all right to make mistakes." And, if the student is having difficulty with a question, I will supply the answer, as long as the test instructions permit this sort of help.

The results of the evaluation and trial teaching help to determine specific goals for a child and develop a system for reaching these goals. If there is sufficient need and time available, I or another specialist may plan to work with the student in the classroom or during pull-out sessions in a reading room. Otherwise, a specialist will map out a plan with the classroom teacher and set up a schedule for the teacher to "check in" with the specialist on a regular basis.

Conferring With A Student & The Student's Parents

The next step is to discuss the results of the evaluation and trial teaching with the student and the student's parents. Of course, how this is done can have a powerful influence on the attitude and performance of the child.

When talking with the child, a reading specialist usually praises areas in which the student has done well and talks about teaching methods that will help the child strengthen weaker skills. The level of detail during this discussion depends on the age and maturity of the child, but overall the conversation is often quite encouraging for the child, who realizes that overcoming problems and learning to read well is possible.

During the meeting with the student's parents, the specialist reviews the results of the evaluation and trial teaching, discusses the child's reading difficulties, and presents plans for remediation. I find it helpful to stress the idea of a parent-school partnership and offer some practical suggestions for supporting the learning process at home. This might include spending time together on appropriate, enjoyable books and games, and helping the child with reading assignments from school.

I talk to parents about the value of reading together as a family activity and emphasize how proud children feel when they read to their parents. I remind them that the books should not be too difficult, so the children can read with very few errors. I also discuss how important it is for parents to read to their children, even after the children have learned how to read, as this fosters children's imaginations. Also, parents sometimes choose books that their children might not pick up by themselves, but which the children then end up learning from and enjoying. Finally, I explain the idea of "patterning" and how important it is for children to see their parents reading to obtain information and enjoyment.

I also emphasize that reading does not always have to be done with books. Encouraging a child to read magazines, game manuals, and other sorts of printed material is important and may spark an interest in a particular subject—or in reading in general —that has been missing in the past.

Implementing An Effective Reading Program

Having tested, evaluated, and conferred, the reading specialist now implements a learning plan designed to improve the child's reading ability so as to meet the grade-level expectations at the child's school. Essentially, this plan will be an age-appropriate program that integrates literature and phonics in a way that helps the child become an enthusiastic and competent reader.

Knowing that students' needs change, the reading specialist's plan covers just the next few months, rather than a whole year. Specialists usually re-evaluate their students in a semi-formal way every three months. Often, this is done when school reports are due or parent conferences are scheduled. Another natural re-assessment time is when specialists confer with the students' classroom teachers.

If a plan is not producing the desired results, the specialist needs to be flexible enough to alter her approach. At the same time, the specialist must also continue working in an organized, systematic way, in order to meet the different needs of a wide range of students and teach them all effectively. The following tools and techniques have helped me and many other reading specialists implement this sort of balanced approach and achieve our teaching goals:

1. Build A Personal Bond

Establishing a strong, positive relationship with a student is a vital element of successful reading instruction. This sort of relationship encourages a student to try harder and to feel comfortable enough to risk making a mistake. A strong, personal bond has become even more important now than it used to be, because so many of today's children come from home environments where these sorts of bonds are not being forged the way they were in the past.

2. Create A Student File

Once I begin working with a student, I set up a file folder for that child. In it, I keep a checklist identifying the skills that the child needs to learn, which are then checked off as they are mastered. Throughout the year, I refer back to this checklist and use it when working and conferring with the student.

This file is also where I keep samples of the student's writing, including work done at the beginning of the school year, Christmas, spring, and the end of the year. These samples can be particularly helpful during conferences with parents and with the student, all of whom can see the progress that has occurred. This is usually very gratifying and serves as an incentive for further effort.

3. Record Students' Oral Reading

I also keep a cassette tape containing samples of a student's oral reading at four or five points during the school year. Like the writing samples, the tape documents the student's progress and can be very helpful during conferences, because it shows how much the student has achieved.

4. Maintain A "Reading Plan" Notebook

One item that I absolutely depend on is a notebook containing dated lesson plans for each of my reading groups. I leave ample space after each day's plans, so I can jot down comments about each child's progress and note specific events. This becomes another important and accurate source of information when evaluating a child's progress, because it shows exactly when a child was having difficulty or improving in a particular area. In order to work with several reading groups effectively, I recommend using a loose leaf notebook that can be divided into separate sections for each group.

5. Use Games

Educational games can be an incredibly effective teaching tool, because even the most reluctant learners are eager to participate when they feel they can play the games successfully. Games make repetitive but necessary tasks enjoyable and so can help strengthen students' phonic skills, language skills, and sight vocabulary, as well as social skills.

Games can also be used over and over again in different ways. The same basic game board can be used by different students at different times, and in some cases the words or other features can be changed as needed, so the same students can use them in new ways. Other games may only be used to teach certain skills, but can be used year after year for the same purpose.

When parents ask what they can do to help their children with reading, I often recommend particular games or even send games home with the children. The games can become an enjoyable and relatively stress-free way to work on reading, and parents are often delighted to know they are helping their children in this way.

6. Use Incentives

Like adults, children enjoy being rewarded for genuine effort and good work, and I have found that incentives can contribute to both individual and group achievement. With individual children, I may offer stickers or a choice from a prize box containing a variety of interesting and unusual items. I establish a point system in which a good day's work is worth a point, and after a child achieves a certain number of points, he or she gets to choose a prize. When I want to reward an entire reading group for reaching a goal, I may offer extra time for reading games, a special activity, or an ice cream or pizza party.

7. Create A Personalized "Reading Room"

A room in which students learn to read should provide an inviting and supportive environment. Yet, a reading specialist may have her own room, "float" to different rooms that become available, or work with each student in his or her own classroom. Whatever the set-up—and I have worked with all of the above—the specialist must do what she can to create an appropriate environment.

A specialist fortunate enough to have her own room can simply fill it with items that encourage children to read and also help them feel comfortable and secure. For example, a basketball poster that combines eye-catching graphics with text and statistics usually elicits great interest. Sometimes, I bring in one of my own stuffed animals and display it with an accompanying story that explains its history. Then, I encourage children to bring in their own favorite stuffed animals, write about them, and put their animals and stories on display. This prompts children to read what they and others have written, and it can lead to other writing projects—such as describing the world from their animals' point of view—which will also become interesting reading material.

Samples of children's work should always be prominently displayed, both to support the children who did the work and stimulate interest among others. Most classroom teachers also recognize the importance of this and use parts of their walls and bulletin boards for this purpose. One teacher I know has a "Student of the Week" board, where each child in the class has a turn to be featured. The display includes a current photo and baby photo of the child, information about hobbies and favorite sports, and other personal details, as well as a story written by the child. Naturally, the children like to read about themselves and each other.

Children's love of special occasions can also stimulate interest in reading. Thought-provoking holiday and seasonal decorations can stimulate or tie-in with reading projects. For example, a picture of a child telling a department store Santa what he or she wants for Christmas offers endless story possibilities. And, a school's art teacher usually has a portfolio of prints which include seasonal pictures and additional subject matter that can be linked to reading and writing. Some teachers even create "art galleries" where pictures are displayed with accompanying stories, shoe-box dioramas, or other related creations of the student.

Doing all this as a traveling specialist is more difficult but can be accomplished. When I have to float from room to room, I carry important items—even including stuffed animals—in a bag, and then use them wherever I'm working with my students. Small, portable bulletin boards can be used in a similar way, or there may be an available bulletin board in the school library or a hallway which the specialist can use to display students' work.

8. Use Stimulating Objects & Materials

"Concrete" objects that children relate to and remember can help them learn phonics. To cite just one example, many children learn the *sh* sound quickly when it is taught in conjunction with a model *ship* they can examine. And, because students are curious about their teachers' lives outside of school, they are especially interested in things teachers bring in from their own homes.

Other things that spark children's interest or curiosity can also help them learn. For example, sometimes I bring in a fancy shopping bag and show it to a group before they read a story. I tell them there is something inside the bag that will be mentioned in the story, and they have to pay close attention as we read together, so they can guess what is in the bag. After the story has been read, the students can offer their guesses and then examine what is in the bag, which often leads to further discussion of the object and the story.

Unfortunately, not all of a teacher's materials can be interesting, but often they can be made more appealing. Something like putting flash cards in a special box, or using colored index cards instead of plain white ones, can help some children overcome resistance they may have to working with these sorts of materials.

9. Build Interest & Self-Esteem With Books

When children have reading material that is interesting and appropriate for them, they feel successful as readers and often become more enthusiastic about the reading process. This was brought home to me again recently when I assigned David, a third grader with dyslexia, a very short mystery book to read independently at home. He was obviously reluctant to take the book home and, sure enough, the next day he told me he hadn't had time to read the story. I accepted the excuse but urged him again to try reading the book. When I asked him about it the following day, his face lit up and he said, "It wasn't really so bad to read it." He then made my day by asking whether I had any other books by the same author.

Reading Remediation

Using the tools and techniques just described, the reading specialist proceeds to implement a balanced program that combines the reading of children's literature with systematic phonics instruction, including "decoding" and "encoding" activities. (Essentially, decoding is the process of sounding out or otherwise reading written words, while encoding is the process of spelling and writing words.)

In most cases, the first step for a specialist working with a large number of students at one time is organizing the students into reading groups, based on data from their evaluations. An ideal reading group has no more than five students in it, but the actual number is determined by the particular school system.

The way in which the group is taught depends both on the specialist and the group. Some specialists have completely individualized work programs for each of the students, who rarely work together. In order for the specialist to have this sort of time with individual students, the others must have suitable and interesting reading material—or other work—that encourages their efforts and holds their attention. Other specialists have the students work together on some projects and then individually on others. During the time when the children are working independently, the specialist spends a few minutes with each child, perhaps teaching a new phonics rule or reviewing some work the child has already done.

Like many specialists, I base my approach on the current needs of the students, teaching the group as a whole when they have similar needs, and working individually with students as much as possible when their needs are different. Another consideration is how best to teach different information and skills. When teaching phonics, I find that children learn best if a variety of methods and materials are used to teach a particular sound or phonetic rule. So in addition to printed materials, I use a number of different games that reinforce particular skills or information. With beginning readers, I also make use of pictures drawn by the students themselves. For each particular phonetic sound, each student decides on a picture that he or she associates with the sound. (Older students decide on a word.)

For example, when learning the *ch* sound, a student may choose *church* as a key word. The student writes *ch* on the front of the index card and draws a picture of a church on the back of the card. This card then remains in the student's personal Word Box, and each day I show the student the front of the card. Without looking at the back of the card, the student is supposed to say the name of the picture and then the sound of the letter combination. If the student can do this, I put a check mark on the card, and when a student can do it five days in a row, I consider the understanding of this sound-symbol correspondence "automatic" and put the card in the back of the Word Box, to be reviewed a few months later. (I like to make sure that a sound or rule has become automatic before we go on to a new one, and over the years I have found that my five-check system is very effective in this regard, because it enables me to clearly see whether a child has achieved mastery.)

Some children need a more multi-sensory approach, however, and this is where games can be especially helpful. To help a tactile/kinesthetic learner, I have found the game known as "Pat, Pat, Clap, Clap," can be used in a variety of ways (thanks to my son and his teacher, Barbara Juhel, for this). For example, when teaching the *oo* sound, I write *oo* on the chalkboard and ask students to try to think of words that have this sound. I warn them to try to think of a few words, in case someone else chooses one they have thought of. When they are ready, I start by saying the name of the game and simultaneously patting my thighs twice and clapping my hands twice, then saying an *oo* word: "Pat, Pat, Clap, Clap, *broom*." Each child then has a chance to do the same with his or her *oo* word. If room is available, it can be even more fun to do this sitting in a circle.

The old game, "Grandmother's Trunk," is a good way to reinforce a sound auditorially. I tell the students that Grandmother is packing a trunk and all the items in it have an *oo* sound. Everyone thinks up appropriate words, and I start by saying something such as, "In Grandmother's trunk there is a *stool*." Then, each student has to use the same phrase with the *oo* word(s) that came before, as well as adding their own: "In Grandmother's trunk, there is a *stool* and a *tool*." In addition to focusing the students on specific sounds, this game helps them develop their auditory memories. With some groups, it may be fun for children who cannot think of a word to be considered "out," but with other groups this can become too competitive.

Some children learn better when they have something that they can feel and see while sounding out words. These children may benefit from a program called Auditory Discrimination in Depth (see the Resource Section), which uses differently colored blocks to develop auditory conceptualization skills in conjunction with any reading program. The colored blocks can be used to identify specific sounds, enabling children to see the location and sequence of the sounds they hear. For example, a specialist might say, "Show me *zup*," and the student would lay out three differently colored blocks. Then, the specialist might say, "Show me *zud*," and the student would remove the last block, replacing it with a block of a different color. Once a student is able to do this, tiles featuring individual letters are added to the process, and later the students begin writing the letters themselves.

In addition to working on phonics in ways such as this, a reading specialist must also help her students develop reading comprehension skills. How she does this depends on her students' reading comprehension levels, as well as how the specialist chooses to run her particular program.

With beginning readers, I introduce reading comprehension skills as soon as the students can read a short, little phonics book aloud. I discuss the story with them, and as they become more proficient readers, my questions become more detailed, while the material I ask them to read becomes more varied. I start with the basic comprehension skills of finding the main idea and the important details of a passage, and then using this information to draw a conclusion. At first, I demonstrate each skill, and we practice the skill together. After sufficient work has been done, I ask the students to do some independent exercises, which I later review with them, either as a group or individually.

Realizing that skills alone are not enough, a reading specialist also carefully chooses a variety of material to read aloud to her students, and for older students to read independently. This not only fosters an interest in reading, it helps build important skills. For example, students interested in what they are hearing tend to listen more carefully, improving their auditory discrimination and memory—two capabilities which have become extremely important in today's society but tend to be taken for granted. So, in addition to reading aloud appropriate books, a specialist may also read poetry and timely, thought-provoking articles from newspapers and magazines, in order to provide important, multi-faceted support for the reading process.

There's More To It Than Just Reading

Knowing how closely reading, writing, and other aspects of language development are connected, a reading specialist also integrates writing and language development with reading instruction.

For example, writing a well-organized story requires students to use some of the same techniques used by successful readers, such as thinking about an incident and deciding what is important about it. So, as soon as possible, a reading specialist encourages her students to write stories, perhaps assigning a particular topic, or allowing the students to write either a creative story or a factual story about an experience they select. This material can then also serve as something to be read silently or aloud.

I like to give each student his or her own "Story Notebook." With younger students, I write the start of each story in the notebook, and then the children take over. The stories tend to be short at first, but the children become very pleased when they realize they have actually written a story and can read it themselves.

Formal paragraph writing is introduced when students' skills are sufficiently developed—usually during the second half of second grade. Then, by the end of second grade, a fair number of children may be able to write a very basic paragraph consisting of a topic sentence, three supporting sentences, and a concluding sentence. By the end of third grade, some students will have learned how to plan and write an extended paragraph.

This sort of writing parallels and supports work on reading comprehension skills. As students learn how to plan and construct a paragraph, identifying the main idea and turning it into a topic sentence is emphasized again and again. This is very similar to having young readers practice finding the main idea in a paragraph they have read. In this and other ways, the teaching of reading and writing truly becomes integrated.

When evaluating a child's writing, the reading specialist considers two key questions. The first is whether the sentence structure, language usage, and spelling are appropriate for the student's current grade level. Any areas that need additional help should be noted—and carefully written down, especially if the child also needs work on his or her handwriting.

The second question is whether too many corrections will make a student feel inhibited, or whether the student will be dissatisfied if corrections are omitted. I believe the extent of the corrections should depend on the individual needs and preferences of each student. For example, James, a first grader who had a winning smile and difficulties with reading and writing, frequently worried and asked at least once during each session, "Is it right?" When we reviewed his work, I only pointed out some of the more basic mistakes. Mark, on the other hand, was a self-confident second grader who had dyslexia. He tended to be a perfectionist and took his schoolwork very seriously, wanting to know all his errors and taking great pleasure in reviewing a corrected paper.

With both students, I made sure to praise their work and asked them to read it aloud. I wanted them to realize that writing a thought down enables them to read it, and that writing and reading are closely linked in this way. This may seem obvious to adults, but some children do not automatically make this connection.

In addition to developing students' reading and writing skills, a reading specialist also helps to develop students' language and vocabulary skills, which play an important role in reading comprehension. In particular, young readers need to become familiar with synonyms, antonyms, and word categorization.

This can occur orally, through written assignments, and through games. For example, the specialist may write a word on a blackboard or chart and then ask the students to think of words that have the same meaning. The specialist makes a list of appropriate suggestions, which then become vocabulary words for the students who are unfamiliar with them. The list can remain up for days, with new words being added as students think of them. Categorization can be taught as a writing assignment in a similar way, with small groups of younger children creating lists based on physical characteristics (i.e., *round* things) and older students creating lists based on more abstract characteristics such as a purpose or action (i.e., *tools*).

My students enjoy a language skills activity based on the *Mad Libs* books available at many toy stores. These books contain stories in which key words are left out. In order to fill in the blank, students must be able to comprehend the stories and think of appropriate words. I like to write a story on the board which has several words missing, but instead of asking for parts of speech, I ask for a "describing" word or an "action" word. (Once third graders are comfortable with this activity, I introduce grammatical terms such as *noun, verb, adjective,* and *adverb.*) After the words have been filled in, my students take turns reading the story aloud or do so together. A few weeks later, I often use the same story again, and the children enjoy thinking of different words to use. Then, we read and compare both versions of the story.

Vocabulary development is also supported through the reading of varied materials. New words often seem more interesting when presented in the context of a story or other appropriate reading material. To make sure new words are understood and remembered, I like to discuss unknown words before something is read and then review them again afterwards.

Supporting Students By Supporting Their Teachers

A reading specialist's students are also being taught by classroom teachers, so maintaining close communication with those teachers is another important part of the specialist's job. The specialist offers suggestions and appropriate materials for the students to use in the classroom, and—by listening to the insights of the classroom teacher—the specialist learns more about the students' needs and progress.

The specialist can also serve as a school's reading resource in a more general way. She can answer questions about teaching techniques, the reading levels of books, and particular students. She can also make her materials available as school-wide resources. When I was a graduate student, a professor suggested that my fellow students and I always walk around our schools with a large bag containing materials that we would be ready to lend to teachers. This benefits all concerned, because the initial loan of a book or other material can help to develop a long-term, working partnership between educators, in addition to helping an individual student.

Adapting A Reading Specialist's Strategies & Techniques

As you have probably noticed while reading the preceding pages, a classroom teacher can and often does use similar strategies and techniques to teach children to read. And, while a classroom teacher may not have the same extensive training as a reading specialist, the teacher often does have both the ability and need to use a similar approach in order to help students learn. Here's a brief overview of how you can do this in a systematic way.

Like a reading specialist, you start by evaluating all your students when the school year begins. Meeting with each student individually for a brief time, you ask some general questions and administer a series of short evaluations that provide a clear picture of your students' current reading skills. Third grade teachers can also use a quick auditory comprehension test, and then have an entire group or class complete a reading comprehension test.

Once you have the results of your evaluations, it's time to consider and compare them, and then divide your class into reading groups. Essentially, you end up with three major categories of current ability levels—high, middle, and low—which today might be called advanced, mid-range, and emerging, or some other characterizations of your choice. Depending on your class size and make-up, you may have just three groups or need to divide the students into even smaller groups, in order to meet students' individual needs more efficiently.

It is very important *not* to label the students as having low or average ability, because this can become an excuse or a self-fulfilling prophecy. And, knowing that students' skills and abilities change during the course of the school year, you should informally re-evaluate individual students every few months and change the groups when appropriate.

The reading groups meet for about an hour and a half every morning. While you're working with one group or its members, your other students have a variety of group or independent assignments to complete. I provide each child with a "learning packet" containing assignments and materials which are updated frequently. Changing the tasks regularly helps the students practice different skills and learn more. It also keeps the work more interesting. (Each of the following chapters on grades 1-3 contains sample learning packet materials.)

Of course, it may take time for your students to learn to work independently. During the first few weeks of school, many of the assignments may have to be done as a whole-class activity. This can happen while you are still in the process of evaluating your students and forming the initial reading groups. Then, the transition to independent work can occur as the groups begin meeting on a daily basis. And, as noted earlier, classroom aides or parent volunteers can also provide assistance with reading, especially if some children continue to have difficulty working independently.

In addition to your work with the reading groups in the morning, you act as a reading specialist in other ways throughout the day. You or your students may read something aloud at different times, including materials from other subject areas such as science, social studies, or math. Your students should also have opportunities to read silently, with your help in selecting books, learning new words, and making progress in other ways, as well. Work on writing assignments that are then read aloud also contributes to the reading process, as do reading parties and authors' teas—special events that promote the importance and enjoyment of reading. You can also offer and receive assistance when coordinating with parents and other educators who work with your students.

In sum, as your own reading specialist, you continue to evaluate your students over time and respond to their individual needs, while providing a balanced program that includes systematic phonics and skills instruction, silent and oral reading of appropriate children's literature, and work on writing, vocabulary, listening, and other aspects of language development. As much as possible, you individualize the strategies and techniques to meet the needs of specific students, and you work effectively with the other adults in the children's lives who are directly involved in supporting the learning process.

Getting There From Here

The next three chapters provide more detailed information about using this approach in grades 1-3. In addition to reading the chapter about your own grade, you may want to review the information about grades above and/or below yours, as you are likely to find some suggestions that prove helpful with advanced or lagging students. Also, many of the techniques build on ones used in previous grades, which may be referred back to rather than repeated in each chapter.

After the three grade-level chapters, you'll find a chapter that provides information about teaching students who have special needs. Then, following chapters provide information about implementing a team approach with colleagues and parents, and dealing with the impact of today's media on young readers. A final section identifies books and other learning resources appropriate for students in grades 1-3, as well as professional resources for educators.

It is my hope and belief that all this information will enable you to:

1. successfully meet the needs of your full range of students,

2. work more effectively with colleagues and your students' parents,

3. experience more professional and personal satisfaction in your classroom.

CHAPTER 3

Becoming A First Grade Reading Specialist

I love to watch first graders during the first few days of the school year. They look so neat and expectant, and often they are wearing something new that they are delighted to show you. They feel proud of themselves and for now, at least, they usually try hard and are on their best behavior.

First graders seem to realize this is an important year for them. If you ask them about first grade, often they will tell you that first grade is when you learn to read and write.

First grade teachers usually share this expectation and also have some other expectations of their own. They know their students must start to develop basic reading, writing, language, and auditory skills, but they also want their students to develop a love of reading and books. And, they want this crucial year to be filled with positive experiences and meaningful accomplishments, so that the students will continue to have positive feelings about school and themselves.

Obviously, this is a pretty tall order, but I believe it can be accomplished through an organized, sequential reading program. By evaluating students effectively and then providing a mixture of whole-class, small-group, and individualized instruction, today's first grade teachers can teach the wide range of students in their classrooms to read well and enthusiastically.

At the start of first grade, classroom teachers usually find some big differences in the reading abilities of their students. Some students may not be able to read simple words, while others can read short books. Some children know the names of letters but virtually no corresponding sounds; others can recognize rhyming pairs. Most first graders have at least one favorite story they like to have read to them, and a number of the "readers" will have memorized part or all of their favorite stories. Other students may not be able to do this but are familiar with a few key sight words.

Once you have identified the range of readers in your classroom, you can plan effective instructional strategies and organize the students into reading groups. Then, you'll be able to implement an integrated approach that combines lots of practice reading with phonics instruction, story time, and other language development activities.

As part of this process, you need to establish your basic reading routines, which will continue with some variation throughout the school year. You have to explain to your students what you expect them to do while you are working with other students, and you have to show them how to use the various materials that support the development of reading skills. I find it helpful at the start of the year to role-play different problems that may occur when students are working without my direct supervision, and from then on I only add new activities after introducing them to the whole class or a particular reading group.

The remainder of this chapter shows in more detail how first grade teachers can successfully become their own reading specialists. After explaining how to use and interpret the evaluations included in this chapter, I discuss setting up reading groups and helping students function effectively in them. Then, I review the elements of the reading program that I believe should be taught in first grade, in order to help students become enthusiastic readers. Following sections of this chapter provide suggestions for teaching writing—as well as language and auditory skills—in first grade.

Evaluating Your Incoming First Graders

Knowing that the children who enter your classroom have a variety of abilities and educational backgrounds, you need more than just the information passed along by their kindergarten teachers. And, given your busy schedule and numerous priorities during the first few weeks of school, you need a relatively quick way to obtain the information you need, so that you can get right to work on organizing and teaching such a wide range of students effectively.

The reproducible Reading Readiness Evaluation included in this section is designed to help you accomplish these goals. This informal evaluation, which takes only a few minutes with each student to complete, is easy to interpret and provides information about a first grader's general knowledge, grapho-motor skills, reading readiness, and reading skills. It includes some general questions, a handwriting sample, and a series of short tests that reveal a child's rhyming skills, understanding of the alphabet, and knowledge of phonics and sight words.

Reading Readiness Evaluation

For durability I suggest that you mount the different parts of the test on large index cards.

Naming Lower Case Letters

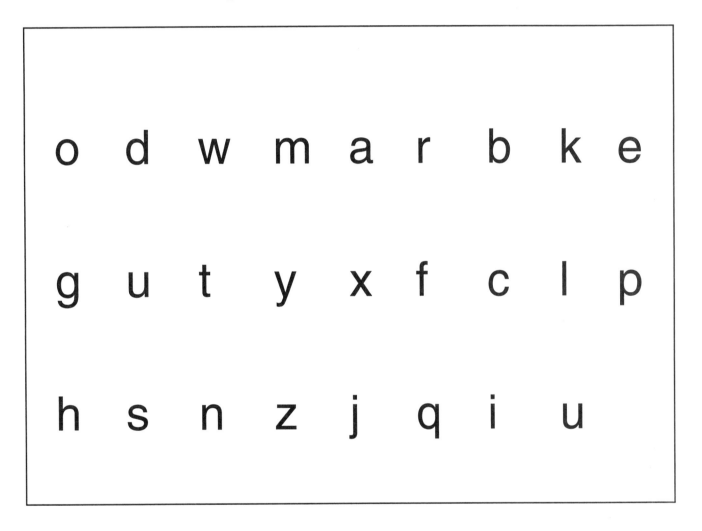

Naming Capital Letters

E U X Z F G S O

W Q A K C L B H P

I J D Y M V R N T

Saying Letter Sounds

c d n f s t p

b l k r x j y

w m q h v g z

Reading Words

Tests 5-8

cap	pin	red	rob	mug

date	fine	note	cube	Pete

heel	leak	sail	hay	goal

see	was	to	book	green
work	laugh	house	seven	two

Reading Readiness Evaluation - Student Record Sheet

Student's Name: _____

Date: _____

Date of Birth: _____

I. General Information Questions:

1. When is your birthday? _____

2. What is your address? _____

3. What is your telephone number? _____

Teacher Comments:

II. Handwriting Sample:

Teacher Comments:

III. Reading Readiness and Early Reading Skills

1. Naming Lower Case Letters
   Letters Missed: _____
   Number Correct: _____

2. Naming Capital Letters
   Letters Missed: _____
   Number Correct: _____

3. Rhyming Test
   Sample: "Can you tell me a word that rhymes with cat?" Supply the answer if necessary. Then proceed in a similar manner with the test words.

   1. man   _____
   2. bad   _____
   3. bake   _____
   4. cap   _____
   5. bike   _____
   Number correct: _____

4. Giving Letter Sounds
   Letters Missed: _____

   Number Correct: _____

5. Short Vowel Words
   Errors: _____

   Number Correct: _____

6. Magic e Words
   Errors: _____

   Number Correct: _____

7. Two Vowels Together Words
   Errors: _____

   Number Correct: _____

8. Sight Words

1. see _____	6. work _____
2. was _____	7. laugh _____
3. to _____	8. house _____
4. book _____	9. seven _____
5. green _____	10. two _____

   Number Correct: _____

   Teacher Comments:

To prepare for the test, you'll want to have one (or more, depending on class size) class summary sheet, which has a row for each student's name and then a column for each of the assessments you will be administering during the school year. You'll also need a copy of each test card and sufficient copies of the individual Student Record Sheets, as well as paper and pencils for the students to use.

I keep the Student Record Sheet in front of me while administering the evaluation, so I can write down any incorrect answers or pertinent remarks the student makes. When completed, this sheet accurately documents how the student was functioning at the start of the year. I like to review it with parents during the first conference in the fall, and I keep it in the child's file all year.

You know the best times for working individually with students in your classroom, but in my experience a good time is when the children are engaged in assigned "seat work" or quiet play. I sit off to one side with the child being assessed and start with the general information questions listed on page 29. I find I can learn a lot by asking a few questions as basic as, "What is your birthday?" In order to answer this sort of question, a child has to retrieve information and put it in sequence, which is an important skill for reading and other areas of the first grade curriculum.

Next, I ask the student to write his or her name on a piece of paper, which I later date and keep in the child's file. Most children entering first grade are eager to write their names, having been taught by a family member or kindergarten teacher to write their first—and, sometimes, their last—name. When children write only their first name, I ask if they can write their last name or any letters in it.

The simple act of writing a name can be quite revealing. The way in which each student grips the pencil should be noted, and the letter formation and spacing on the page provide information about grapho-motor skills, especially when compared with the writing of other students. For example, is the letter formed, starting at the correct point and staying within the lines? And, does the writing look shaky or pressured? This information gives you a sense of how much work on handwriting will be needed. Also, the ability to write the last name is often a good indication of the strength of a child's visual memory.

Next come the reading-related questions, which provide you with a quick, diagnostic evaluation that shows whether a child has learned important readiness and reading skills. The questions cover the gamut from the basic to the more advanced skills for first graders, and so can be a very useful resource in today's diverse classrooms.

As mentioned in the previous chapter, I always tell the students that their work will help me by giving me a better idea of what they did in kindergarten and what we should do together in first grade. Also, I always say that I do not expect the students to know everything I ask.

During the test, I try to keep the children interested and relaxed, praising their efforts even though the actual performance may be weak. If it is weak, I might make a comment such as, "That's almost right. Try it again."

The first task for the student is to identify the lower case letters of the alphabet, a skill that is usually practiced often in kindergarten. I point to the first letter on the card and ask, "Can you tell me what letter this is?" If there's any hesitation, I give the child a few moments to think, and if he or she has difficulty with numerous letters, I may switch to upper case letters, which are easier to identify.

The child's responses provide baseline information about his or her progress in learning the alphabet, and show whether and where intensive review of the lower case letters is needed. I would expect a first grader to know all of the lower and upper case letters, although confusion about *n* and *u* or *b, d,* and *p* are still common at this age.

The rhyming test (see item 3 on the Student Record Sheet) asks students to supply a word that rhymes with a given word. I ask, "Can you tell me a word that rhymes with *cat*?", and if the student cannot answer correctly, I supply a rhyming word and then ask the student to think of a rhyme for the next word. Rhyming is important because it reveals whether a child can identify similar sounds—a key indicator of a child's ability to learn phonics. Children who have trouble with rhyming may need to rely more on a sight word approach, although they should also be taught phonics, which will probably "click" for them at a later age.

After the rhyming test, each student is asked to identify consonant sounds. This skill is also taught in many kindergartens, so at least some students are likely to be able to do it. First graders who have difficulty answering any of these questions are likely to need a lot of assistance, including extra lessons and activities focused on the consonants. This part of the evaluation also provides important information in regard to placement in reading groups, as students who need intensive work on consonants should be in a different group from the students ready to proceed with the short vowel sounds.

In the second section of this evaluation, you ask the students to read actual words, presenting the words much as you did the letters of the alphabet. This section shows whether a child can decode words phonetically (although some words may have been learned as sight words). The words are presented in the usual phonetic order, with the short vowel words first. Then come long vowel words that a child must decode using the "magic *e*" rule, followed by long vowel words that require use of the "two vowels together" rule. A final series of words reveals whether each student can recognize some basic sight words.

Remember that incorrect answers can be very informative and should be noted on the Student Record Sheet. For example, if a child reads *rib* for *rob*, you have learned that the child knew the first and last part of the word, but not the vowel sound. It's also important to note how the child "attacked" the word. Did he or she try to sound a word out, rely on sight memory, or just take a guess. This can help to determine a child's learning style, because, for example, phonics may be the best approach with a child who tries to sound out a word. Another child who knows some sight words may be a natural sight word reader or may just not have been introduced to phonics in kindergarten. Write down your impressions, and be ready to ask some follow-up questions.

When a child can read a few words, I ask where he or she learned to read. A child may have been taught some words in kindergarten, or picked them up from reading signs or ads, or been shown sight words by a parent at home. This can provide valuable information about a child's previous training or instinctive way of learning.

Setting Up & Working With Your Reading Groups

Reading groups are an important and effective way to teach and review a variety of vital reading skills. Part of the time is spent introducing or reviewing phonic skills, which are then reinforced by a daily dictation. Children also take turns reading a story, which is then discussed, and new sight words are introduced and reviewed. Usually, I finish a session with a game that reinforces the phonic skill I am teaching. Of course, this format is not written in stone, so other activities can be added or substituted as needed.

Organizing your students into reading groups based on ability levels provides a number of important benefits. A small reading group provides you with a more detailed understanding of the progress made by individual children, and this knowledge can help you focus on specific needs. Students also receive more individualized attention in a small group, and because all the students in the group have similar needs, what you teach and what they practice is more likely to be relevant to each member of the group, which results in the students being more "tuned in" to the work. This also makes the students more likely to develop a sense of confidence and accomplishment in regard to reading.

Some educators prefer relying solely on mixed groupings, instead. While I believe mixed groupings should be used and encouraged during the school day, because they also provide important benefits, I have found that this approach becomes counter-productive and frustrating for children during reading instruction. The more able students grow bored, and the less able often feel incompetent and defeated. My recommendation, therefore, is to group the students initially on the basis of their current academic profiles, as shown by the results of the evaluation described above.

The optimum number of children in a group is five or six, and eight should be the maximum number. Otherwise, the group becomes too large for you to teach effectively. Ideally, you would just have three reading groups, but because of increased class sizes, you may need to have four, in which case you would need to increase the amount of independent work you assign and lengthen the amount of time devoted to playing educational games.

Another option is to add another thirty-minute reading period to your schedule. This time could be used for additional time at a reading center, or work on a special reading project, or interdisciplinary projects that might include artwork or some other form of self-expression. For example, if students are studying dinosaurs, they could read books about dinosaurs with a friend, and then write and illustrate their own books about dinosaurs. Finally, they could read their books aloud as part of a special presentation, and the books could then remain part of the classroom library for a while.

I prefer to have my reading groups work together early in the morning, right after the whole class morning routine, because this is the most productive time for most children. But, I make sure to rotate the sequence in which I see different groups, so they are not slotted into a specific order every day. And, sometimes I base the order on the group's activities for that day. As noted in the previous chapter, the groups don't necessarily stay the same, because I also make sure to re-evaluate children's needs and the group dynamics from time to time.

When considering which children to include in a group, remember that the group members will need to be able to work together without your direct supervision. With this in mind, I believe there are two fundamental characteristics to consider: reading ability and temperament. Obviously, you would like each member of a group to be at about the same level as all the other members of the group. However, some children who have similar reading abilities may not work well together, which creates a quandary. Do you put them in the same group and hope that they will mature and change their ways, or do you separate them? In my experience, the best answer is to place incompatible children in different groups, rather than spending valuable instructional time dealing with behavior problems. If their personalities or behavior change later in the year, you can always adjust the groups accordingly.

Changes should also be made for other reasons, as well. Some first graders may achieve breakthroughs or rapid improvements which make them better suited for another group. Other children may start to experience difficulties in one group, and after observing and working with them for a few days, you may decide they would fare better in a less advanced group. Even if no dramatic changes have occurred, it's a good idea to take a few minutes every month to evaluate the groups.

For the most part, I find that first graders are very flexible. If you simply tell children that you would like them to switch to a new group because you think it will help them with their work, they will usually accept this. Especially if they see that you make these sorts of changes fairly often, it's not a "big deal," and they will have little or no difficulty making this type of move.

While you spend most of your time introducing and reviewing key reading skills with an entire reading group, at times you assign independent work and then help or evaluate children individually. For example, if a child frequently forgets to stop when he or she comes to the end of a sentence, it's a good time for a reminder and some guided practice. Then, when the child starts to respond appropriately, a demonstration of mastery and some well-deserved praise would be appropriate. Or, if needed progress has not occurred, you may decide that extra help or enrichment is needed.

In addition to your primary role as instructor, you also act as a coach, cheerleader, and salesperson when working with your reading groups. You need to offer support and suggestions that will help your students make progress, and you must also provide the positive feedback that hard work and important accomplishments deserve. You also have to remember that your own interest and enthusiasm help to "sell" reading and the classroom activities that lead to confidence and competence.

"Helping Hands" & Other Management Aids

While three or more reading groups can be managed successfully by a lone teacher, having an aide or parent volunteer available during this time can be of great help to the teacher and the students. As you work with one group or with its members individually, the aide or volunteer can be supervising the other groups and answering any questions about their work.

Older students can also be an excellent source of help, especially for first graders, who usually respond well to help from older children and look forward to these sessions. Many older students also find this sort of activity to be an enjoyable, satisfying experience. One fourth grade boy I know had been doing some tutoring at school but became sick for a few days, so his "younger brother" decided to send a picture and note home to him. The older boy's teacher was kind enough to forward the material , and the teacher later told me the older boy was very pleased and flattered when he received them.

If outside assistance is unavailable, I would set up a cooperative learning plan. This approach includes providing each child with a weekly "reading contract" that he or she agrees to follow. The contract includes a daily schedule and is included in each child's Learning Packet. At the end of the week, children who have fulfilled their contracts are praised for their work and allowed to choose a prize or some other incentive.

In order for this approach to work well, careful planning is needed. I find it helpful to have the highest and lowest groups doing some of their independent work at the same time. Members of the more advanced group can even help members of their own group or another group with their work at times. For example, two children might be responsible for answering questions about Learning Packet assignments, with one handling questions about Story Journals and the other handling questions about the phonic, language, and handwriting sheets.

Other members of the various groups also have jobs, which should be rotated on a regular basis. Two children can be responsible for setting up and putting away the various games. Another student can be in charge of the listening center, helping to tape stories that other students read aloud. This student may have a bell to ring when the reader finishes each page, because children are usually familiar with this sound signaling the end of a page on commercial reading tapes, and they enjoy ringing it themselves.

Whatever combination of plans you use, the basic schedule for your three reading groups requires the children to do one hour of work without your direct supervision, as well as 30 minutes of work under your supervision. Here's a basic schedule showing how the time periods can be arranged for each of the three groups:

Use of Time with Teacher and Learning Packet

Minutes	Group 1	Group 2	Group 3
30	work with teacher	work with Learning Packet: phonics sheets read a short book do language and handwriting work if finished early: · read aloud · look at story, etc.	work with Learning Packet: phonic sheets read a short book do language and handwriting work if finished early: · read aloud · look at story, etc.
30	work with Learning Packet: phonics sheets read a short book do language and handwriting work if finished early: · read aloud · look at story, etc.	work with teacher	Options: Story Notebook games tape a story etc.
30	Options: Story Notebook games tape a story etc.	Options: Story Notebook games tape a story etc.	work with teacher

Creating & Using The Learning Packet

As you can see from this schedule, your students' ability to work independently is vital to the success of this approach. And, the Learning Packet is a key component of each student's independent work.

The Learning Packet contains a set of assignments and materials that each child is expected to complete independently, while you are teaching another reading group. Of course, as noted earlier, most first graders need time to grow used to class routines and learn how to work independently, so for the first few weeks of school, many of the assignments need to be done as whole-class projects.

Once your students grow used to the routine, they should be able to complete most assignments on their own. If they cannot, the assignments should be reviewed to see if they are too long or too difficult. Usually, a child should be able to do 75 to 80 percent of the independent work correctly. Otherwise, it is too defeating.

The Learning Packet can include phonic, language, and handwriting sheets, as well as the child's Story Notebook and an appropriate book for reading. As each child becomes a more proficient reader, more trade books can be included in his or her packet. Here's a typical Learning Packet assignment:

For a student who is just beginning to learn the short *o* sound, you'll want to provide a variety of practice sheets focused on this sound. These can include a sheet where the child has to read two sentences and mark the correct one, a sheet that has the child read some questions and answer yes or no, and a sheet that requires the child to write in a needed word.

Good sources for this type of material include *Explode the Code 1*, *Phonics A and B*, and *Primary Phonics—Workbook 1* (listed in the Resource Section, as are all other books referred to in this book). You can also create your own practice sheets, perhaps linking them to stories or books the class reads. Then, you can photocopy the sheets and keep them on file, so you can use them with other groups and during other years.

Of course, some educators now disdain the use of these sorts of practice sheets, which certainly can be over-used. However, I have found that they are simply a needed part of the learning process for many children, because there is no substitute for focused, repetitive practice. We can try to make such work as creative and relevant as possible, but if we just don't bother with it, many children will have trouble mastering basic skills and information.

For a change of pace, you can ask your students to design their own practice sheets for their reading groups. Just give them a sample of what you want them to do. They can also draw pictures that begin with the short *o* sound, or look for such pictures in magazines or books. This sort of work can be done individually or as a cooperative learning project.

Read the two sentences.
✔ the one that goes with the picture.

Mom sits on a pot.

The fox is in the box.

The big dog is hot.

Is the hog on the map?

Ben has a big rod.

A bug is on a log.

The dog sits on a dad.

Did the man hop to Dan?

Mom will fix the mess.

The dog sits in the sun.

The pup hops on the map.

Al is in a hot tub.

Read the sentences.

Write "yes" or "no".   yes   no

Can a cub sit on a box?   _____   _____

Is a log blue?   _____   _____

Can a hog run on a mop?   _____   _____

Can a man jog at six?   _____   _____

Can a big box yell?   _____   _____

Will a top hit?   _____   _____

Can a rod hop on a fox?   _____   _____

Can Pat fill the box?   _____   _____

Can a cop sit on a box?   _____   _____

Can the tot run to his Dad?   _____   _____

Find the word which goes with the picture and write it on the line.

top   rob   hot   dog   log   mop   pot   box

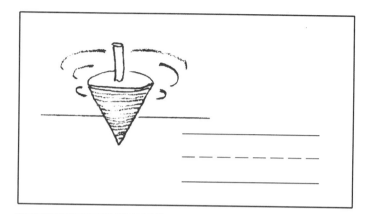

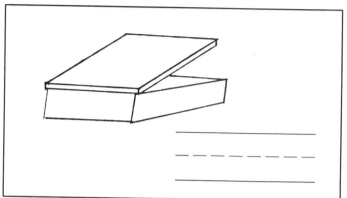

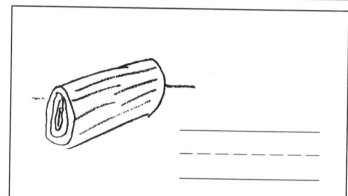

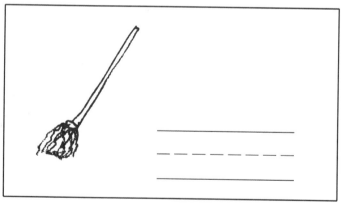

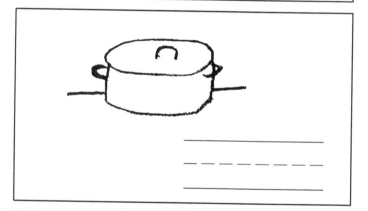

Sample Crossword Puzzle

hope

Jane

rose

make

bake

cake

Pete

five

Dave and the Cake

1. Dave asks _____ to help make a cake.

2. Dave and Jane _____ a cake.

3. They _____ the cake.

4. The _____ is white.

5. On the cake is a _____.

6. They _____ Mom will like the cake.

7. The cake is for _____.

8. He is _____ today.

Sample Crossword Puzzle

eat

cries

goat

weep

Sam

feels

says

eats

name

Joe and Sam

1. Joe has a _____ as a pet.

2. The goat's _____ is Sam.

3. Sam _____ all the plants.

4. Joe _____ , "Sam is bad".

5. He says that _____ will not get a cone.

6. Sam _____ for a cone.

7. Sam _____ Joe is mean and weeps.

8. Joe says, "No need to _____."

9. Do not _____ plants and you will get a cone.

Write the name of the picture.

_____

- - - - - - - - - - - -

_____

- - - - - - - - - - - -

_____

- - - - - - - - - - - -

_____

- - - - - - - - - - - -

_____

- - - - - - - - - - - -

_____

- - - - - - - - - - - -

_____

- - - - - - - - - - - -

_____

- - - - - - - - - - - -

Circle the word that goes with the picture.

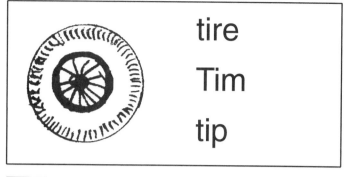
tire
Tim
tip

Coke
cot
cake

Sal
sale
sip

fin
fit
fine

ripe
rip
rut

bit
bill
bike

hop
hog
hope

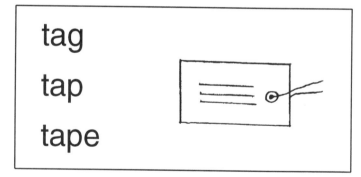
tag
tap
tape

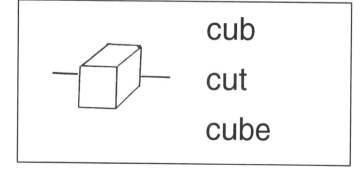
cub
cut
cube

hat
hog
home

Draw a line under the word that matches the picture.

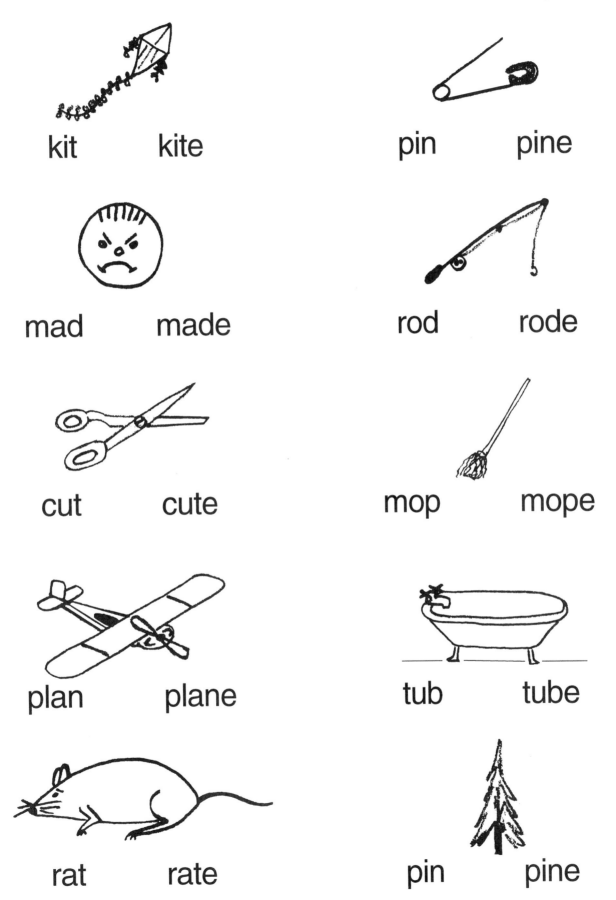

kit   kite

pin   pine

mad   made

rod   rode

cut   cute

mop   mope

plan   plane

tub   tube

rat   rate

pin   pine

I find that having a variety of tasks helps keep first graders focused and is crucial to the success of their independent work. They like practicing a number of skills, and sometimes when I tell a group their time has come to meet with me for thirty minutes, a few will look surprised and say, "What, already?" Then, I know they've had a productive session.

While the students are completing their practice sheets, it helps to have an aide, volunteer, or older student walking around and checking the students' work. Most children like getting quick feedback on their work, such as putting a checkmark on each page and circling any errors, and this makes it easier for you to review their work later.

Remind any helpers that a young child does not always ask for help. Help has to be offered, and usually it is very much appreciated. If other students from your class are helping, you have to decide whether or not they should actually correct their classmates' work. This really depends on how well the children in your class interact, so you have to use your judgment.

After completing their sheets, the children read a short book to themselves, which helps them practice the sound they are learning in their reading group. *Phonics Practice Readers* and *Primary Phonics Story Books* work well for this purpose.

When some children finish their work before the rest of the group, they can choose from a variety of other meaningful educational activities, such as drawing a favorite scene from a story. Children also love hearing themselves read aloud, so another popular activity is choosing a favorite book and taping it, or listening to a tape the child or someone else made. Students may also want to look at a book or magazine in the reading center, and I recommend keeping a set of simple crossword puzzles for them to try there, as well.

During the second thirty minutes of their independent work, the students will have different options. On some days, they complete the assigned language and handwriting sheets from their Learning Packet.

Then, they write in their Story Notebooks (see page 58) and illustrate their stories. Of course, it takes time for many first graders to get used to writing a story, and the stories are often quite short. So, you have to make certain that the children have enough other worthwhile activities to keep them occupied. You might want to set out wooden puzzles that the children can work on by themselves or with a classmate who has also finished. Another option is taping the story the child has just written. First graders also enjoy joke books and may want to write or tape jokes of their own. And, this could be a time when children work on articles for a class newspaper or write a report about a particular event and illustrate it.

When there's room in the schedule, the children can share their stories with each other at the end of reading time. They might either listen as a group or make one tape of all the stories they have just written. A cooperative approach works best when this is done, but if it's not possible, another option is to have the children take turns reading their stories as part of a whole-class activity at a different time during the day.

On other days, the students reinforce their reading skills by reviewing sight words (such as those in the *Dolch Word List*) or playing educational games adapted to focus on particular phonic sounds. Games such as Climb and Slide, Shoot to the Stars, Let's Go Fishing, Robert's Treasure, and Memory are very popular and easy to make. (Instructions are included in the Resource Section.) I prefer games that you make yourselves, because you focus them directly on your first graders' individual needs. However, if you do not have time to do this or need additional ones, a variety of commercial games are available and can prove helpful.

Members of an advanced reading group will not need as much practice strengthening their basic skills. These students can have more time for some of the other activities mentioned above, or they can also work on other projects, such as writing about a book they read or listened to on tape. You can ask them to explain what the story is about or just have them write about a favorite character. Another option is for them to work on a book that they are writing and illustrating themselves.

At the end of the school year, it's gratifying to take a moment and think about how much the members of your reading groups have matured. You will find that most of the first graders learned how to work well independently and in small groups, and they can now accomplish much more in a set period of time. They also take pride in work they have done on their own. And, of course, they have made great progress learning to read and write.

Phonics & Whole Language— An Integrated Approach

After many years of teaching reading, I have come to believe there is no single method that teaches even one first grader to read—much less a whole class of first graders. Instead, first grade teachers need to use a combination of phonics and whole language techniques, because virtually all first graders need exposure to both approaches in order to become successful and enthusiastic readers. As Priscilla Vail explains in her book, *Common Ground: Whole Language & Phonics Working Together*, children need a mixture of the "structure" and "texture" that these approaches provide:

"Structure refers to the nuts and bolts used in assembling or decoding written language. Multisensory phonics instruction provides this solid grounding. Texture refers to the ornamentation which gives language its color, intensity, rhythm, and beauty. Whole language instruction provides texture by soaking children in literature. Structure by itself would be boring, just as free floating texture would be flimsy."

By combining direct instruction in phonics with frequent opportunities to read and enjoy appropriate books, first grade teachers enable their students to gain both the skills and enthusiasm they need. The following sections explain how to teach phonics, encourage reading, and develop other language skills.

Phonics Sequence For The Year

I have found first graders learn phonics best when the material is presented in a particular sequence, starting with the initial consonants. Here's the sequence I recommend:

1. Initial consonants
2. Short vowels
3. Digraphs (*ch, th, sh, wh*)
4. Initial consonant blends
5. Final consonant blends
6. Vowel/consonant endings (*ing, ang, unk, ung, ong, ink, ank*)
7. "Magic *e*" rule, in which the *e* added at the end of a word makes the preceding vowel long (i.e., *lane, bride*)
8. "Two vowels together" rule: when vowels go together, the first one says its name and the second is silent (i.e., *dream*)

The following pages provide detailed explanations of the first two steps, including sample lessons. I'm sure you'll see how the approach I describe can be adapted to the other steps that follow. (Additional suggestions can be found in Nina Traub's book, *Recipe for Reading*.) In addition, I believe you'll also recognize how to adapt this approach to meet the needs of individual students.

Of course, with the variety of children in your class, you may find that some of them have already learned the initial consonants and are ready to focus on short vowel sounds. This is the sort of situation in which reading groups prove so useful. Children who demonstrate their mastery of the initial consonants can be placed in a group which moves right on to the next step.

Teaching Initial Consonant Sounds

Children have to know their consonant sounds before they can begin to decode a word. While some students may have learned this skill in kindergarten, usually there are a number of first graders who don't know all of their consonant sounds initially or need to review them. At the start of the year, when your students are just getting used to the routines of first grade, you may want to do some consonant activities with the entire class. But, once you divide the class into reading groups, you mainly teach this skill to the groups that need it, and this should be done during the morning reading-group time, when your students are more focused.

Introduce each sound along with a "concrete" object, which the children learn to associate with the sound. These objects can be kept in a box and brought out each time that particular sound is mentioned. Using sheets of colored paper, the children who need to work on initial consonant sounds can make their own consonant books under your supervision. Initially, there should be a page for each consonant being learned, but additional pages can be added if a child is having difficulty learning a particular letter. The letter being worked on should appear in the middle of the page, and making the letter out of sandpaper is particularly effective, because it allows the child to feel the letter and see it. If you do not have time to do that or have the children do it, make the letters with a thick magic marker. Have the children add pictures of objects that start with the letter. These can be drawn or cut out of old magazines donated by parents. I store the pages of these consonant books in large envelopes until the books are complete, as they take a while to finish and colored paper tears easily. Finally, I give the children two pieces of colored paper they can make into covers and decorate, and then I help the children assemble their books.

When students are having difficulty with a particular sound, they can also make additional, individual sheets from time to time, using drawn or cut-out pictures. And, they can create collages centered around a particular sound.

Sample Consonant Lesson For A Reading Group

Write the lower-case letter *d* on the board or a chart, and show how it should be formed. Pronounce the sound that *d* makes and then say a few words that begin with it. Next, have the group say the sound along with you. Show the group a toy dog (or whatever other key item you choose), and ask who can think of other words that begin with this sound. Write the words on the board or a chart, and underline the *d* in each word.

Show the children how to form a *d* in the air, using your index and middle finger. It's important for the children to use these two fingers, as this helps them feel the letter through the appropriate muscles. Have them trace the letter on their desk with these fingers (tactile reinforcement), and then have them make the *d* page in their consonant books. Next, they can do a page or two of practice sheets that reinforce the sound you're teaching. For this sort of material, I recommend the *Consonant Book* or *Primary Phonics Programs*.

As the students work, observe how each child functions independently. Children who need help can practice forming the letter on a handwriting sheet, while you reinforce the correct formation. Further practice can occur when the children fill in appropriate handwriting sheets as part of their independent work.

As the year progresses, remember to review consonant sounds that have already been taught, along with the one you are presently teaching. To make this more fun for the students, you can vary how you do it. One way is to put out a few objects associated with sounds that have been studied, and ask for volunteers to tell the group the name of the letter linked to each object and the sound it makes. Then, say a word and ask a child to point to the object that has the same beginning sound.

You can also say a word, have a child come up to the board, say the letter it begins with, and write the letter. Another effective teaching technique is to have the children write (on a blank page of their phonics notebooks) the sound they hear at the beginning of a word. Then, as they learn more consonant sounds, I ask them to write the beginning and ending sounds of a word. Depending on the group, five to eight words should be used for an activity like this.

I always try to end this sort of lesson by reading a short story. (See the Resource Section for some selections.) Children especially enjoy hearing a story during reading group time, perhaps because it is a more personal experience when they are part of a relatively small group. The story can then become the basis for a brief discussion, and as the year goes on, the way in which the children become more adept at discussing stories can be a source of pride and satisfaction for the teacher and students alike.

Consonant Activities For First Graders

Here's a series of projects that help your students practice working with consonants. They can be done with the whole class or a particular reading group. If you have a lot of children who need reinforcement, you might choose to do them both as whole-class and reading-group activities. These activities not only are an effective use of independent reading group time, they can also be constructive time fillers when the class is seated and waiting to go to recess or lunch.

- Using a flashlight to form letters on a wall is usually a very popular activity. At first, you should do it and have the students guess which letter you are making. If they are right, they say the sound it makes and a word that begins with it. After you have done this a few times, ask your students to come up and make letters for their classmates.

- Draw a baseline on a sheet of newspaper, with a dot that signals where to begin each letter, and then have your students use large markers to write a giant version of the letter they are studying. Children love to write large letters, and this is a good grapho-motor exercise. Wrap up the activity by asking the first graders to identify the sound the letter makes, and together write a list of words that begin with this sound.

- Start a "consonant ring," using a notebook ring with index cards or cardboard. Each clue card can have something on it arranged in the shape of the letter. For example, the C card can have cotton balls or candy in shape of a C, while the *D* on the following card is made of colored dots. (This suggestion comes from Priscilla Vail's *Common Ground*, which contains a list of materials that can be used for each letter.)

The children keep these rings at their desks, and can use them for general review or refer to them when they are not sure about a particular sound.

- Tell your students to raise or clap their hands if a word begins with a particular sound. Then, you read aloud a list of words, some of which start with the sound.

- Once the children have learned a few consonants, you can put a few objects or pictures on a table or desk. When you say a sound, a child comes forward to hold up the object or picture that begins with the sound.

- Have the children write down the first letters of a series of words you say. Start with just a few at a time and then build from there.

- Educational games can be an extremely effective way to help students master the consonants. The following section provides more detailed information about using games in this way.

Games For Learning The Consonants

Many students won't know how to play these learning games, so you have to introduce the games in a way that makes playing them a comfortable and enjoyable experience. I would suggest introducing one or two of them before an afternoon choice time early in the year, and then encouraging a few students to play them during choice time. As you won't be working with a reading group then, you'll be able to answer any questions that may arise. In the days that follow, you can explain and provide additional games in a similar way.

Once the children know how to play these games and find them enjoyable, the games become a welcome activity during independent reading group time. And, they can also remain available during choice time, as well. Here's a brief summary of how you can adapt some popular games, which are described in more detail in the Resource Section:

- *Let's Go Fishing* - Put the consonant sounds you are studying on the fish.

- *Robert's Treasure* - The goal is to match three letters together. When a player has three matching letters, he must say a word that begins with the letter before he puts the set down. If he draws a blank, he can use it as a match for any letter that is already in his hand.

- *Consonant Memory* - The children match pairs of pictures, or pairs made up of a letter and a picture that begins with the letter. When a child has a pair, he or she must say the letter, its sound, and the name of the picture.

- *Climb and Slide* - When the child lands on a letter, he must say the sound of the letter and a word that begins with the letter.

- *Shoot to the Stars* - As with Climb and Slide, when the student lands on a letter, he must say the sound of the letter and a word that begins with the letter.

Teaching The Short Vowel Sounds

After the consonant sounds, short vowels are introduced. Usually, this happens in the fall, and how long it takes students to master them depends on the group, as well as how often you teach and review the short vowels. I recommend that you teach or review them daily, because once children have completed this important step in the reading process, they can decode and write an impressive number of words.

Knowing that the children have different starting points and learn at different rates, initially I find it best to do most of this teaching within the reading groups. Then, when most of the class is "into" studying the short vowels, some lessons or review sessions can be done as a whole-class activity. And, by Christmas, you're likely to find that many of your students have learned their short vowels.

The order in which I teach the short vowels is *a, i, u, e, o.* Why? Over the years, I have seen that children find it easier to learn the *a, i,* and *u* sounds, so I introduce them first and then go on to the more difficult ones. As with the consonants, I don't introduce a new vowel sound until their knowledge of the one they are currently studying has become automatic. And, from time to time I make sure to review the ones that have already been mastered.

I love to teach the short vowels, because once children have learned a short vowel—and can decode and read consonant-vowel-consonant words—they are usually so pleased, which I find very gratifying. Of course, some students also feel a great sense of relief. They are the worriers who have been wondering if they will ever be able to read. I'll never forget Alex, who very defiantly said, "I don't read," when I first suggested that we read a simple, phonics-based book together. A short time later, when he painlessly finished reading his first book, he turned to me with a beautiful smile on his face and simply said, "I read it!"

Sample Short Vowel Lesson For A Reading Group

I believe this type of lesson is essential for early reading success, and I would recommend teaching a lesson like it four or five days a week, if possible. In addition, because I believe early morning lessons are the most effective, I would suggest scheduling it for as early in the day as possible. The big question is at what point during the school year you start using this sort of lesson.

Knowing this lesson needs to be done with a particular reading group, because the other students are at different stages of the reading process, you need to determine when each group is ready for it. This can be done by considering the basic order of phonics on page 48, and then looking for mastery of the preceding stage. This sort of ongoing evaluation should continue throughout the school year, with the understanding that some students may be advanced in one particular area, such as phonics, but still need additional help with something else.

The lesson does not have to be followed step-by-step. It can be adapted to the needs of your students, and by simply changing the content, the same format can be used for all the short vowel sounds and for more advanced phonics material.

To introduce a vowel sound, I write the letter on the chalkboard and say the sound of the vowel. Next, I write the letter in the air, using two fingers. I then ask the children to make the letter in the air twice and practice writing it on their desks with their fingers. Together, we think of words that begin with this sound, and I write the words on the chalkboard. This helps reinforce the sound/symbol correspondence.

After that, each child decides on his or her key word. The students draw a picture of their word on one side of a 3" x 5" index card, and either the student or I write the letter on the other side. Each child receives a Word Box with his or her name written on it, and I tell the group they will keep important material in this box for the rest of the year.

On each of the following days, each member of the group will be asked to name the letter and the picture that goes with it, and to say the sound of the letter. When students can do this, a checkmark goes on their card. If a child cannot do it, I simply say that we will look at it again tomorrow. Once the child receives five checks in a row, the sound is considered "automatic" and put in the "automatic" section of the Word Box.

At this point, a student usually asks, "What, for the whole year?" My answer is that I or one of the helpers will re-check each automatic card sometime around Christmas, the February break, and Easter vacation. If a child remembers what is on the card, it can be taken home. Otherwise, the card is put in the front of the box again and will be reviewed regularly until it is automatic once again.

For the next part of the lesson, I introduce a set of flash cards which display a particular "word family," such as the *at* words. I ask the children to say the words, and if most of them can, I will introduce another word family. (After the first lesson of this type, I will also show them the flash cards displaying vowel sounds they have previously learned.) It's always important to praise the children when they can read the words, because they are working hard and deserve positive reinforcement.

Once we are done with the flash cards, the children take out their phonics notebooks and prepare for the daily dictation. (Sample dictations appear below.) This becomes a regular routine, which I try to make a little more appealing by giving out stickers when the dictation is completed. Usually, I dictate six words and a sentence. Sometimes, the sentence is taken from a book we have read together, and then I ask the children which book they think the sentence comes from. I also ask each child to circle the word he or she has written best, as I find this tends to result in neater handwriting.

For the first lesson on a particular vowel, I only use that vowel sound. After the children have had practice writing words and sentences containing this sound, I include words from other vowel families that have already been studied. (To save time compiling these words and sentences, you can refer to *Angling For Words*, its accompanying *Angling For Words (Sentences For Dictation)*, and *Recipe For Reading*.) Following are two sample dictations for the short *a* sound.

When only the *at* and *an* families have been introduced, dictate:

Mat, pan, bat, fan, rat, tan.
Nan and Dan fan Pan.

For a later short *a* lesson when all the short *a* families have been taught, dictate:

Ham, cab, sad, bag, rang, wax.
Sam has a tan bag.

Next comes one of my favorite parts of the lesson—hearing my students read a story aloud. The children love reading from these short phonics books, which we then discuss, and I make sure to praise their efforts. (In some cases, dyslexic students should not be required to read aloud in the group, unless you have previewed the material with them or they volunteer to read.) I would recommend using these phonetic readers until you have covered the entire phonics sequence listed on page 48, although your more advanced group(s) probably won't need to use them after you have introduced the "two vowels together" rule.

I also introduce five sight words a week, starting with the color words and then the Dolch sight words. Before I introduce the color words, I write each one on a large index card and put a line of the color on the other side of the card. I show the word on the front of the card and then turn it over so the children can see the color. Then using the index and middle finger, we write the word in the air, spelling it aloud as we write. Then I line the cards up with the words showing and ask for volunteers to identify each color card. Each child points to a card and then turns it over to check the answer. I go through a similar process with the Dolch words, but to vary the routine, I might write the words on the chalkboard when we first study them, then erase them and write them in a different order, before asking a volunteer to circle the word I say.

These words are also written on index cards for the children and assigned to be studied as homework. I review the cards with individual children either during the reading group time or when the children are doing seat work. An assistant or volunteer can also check them. As with the vowel and consonant cards, a check mark is put on the card when the child correctly identifies it, and when the card has five check marks on it, it is placed in the automatic section of his or her Word Box. The automatic cards are reviewed every few months, and words a student has forgotten are re-learned.

Next, the children complete a page or two in their phonics workbooks. This can be a good time to observe how the children are doing with their workbooks, since most of their workbook assignments are completed while you are teaching a different reading group.

If time permits, I always try to play a short game that reviews the phonic sounds I am currently teaching. For example, if we have studied three vowel sounds, I will make three corresponding columns on the chalkboard, then say a word and ask a child to put a check mark in the appropriate column. A reading group can also be divided into two teams which play this game.

Another popular game is based on a drawing of a tic-tac-toe grid on the chalkboard. I divide the group into the X's and the O's, and then I write a word on the chalkboard. A team member says the word and then can make a mark on the grid.

Finally, no matter what the reading level of the group, I end the lesson by reading a short story or a chapter from a chapter book. This is always an enjoyable part of the lesson.

Vowel Activities & Games For Children

Many of the consonant activities described on pages 50 and 51, such as making consonant rings or drawing large letters on newspaper, can also be adapted to help children learn vowel sounds. These activities and the additional ones described below can be done during reading group time or as a whole-class activity. Children usually enjoy these activities, so they pay attention to them in the morning or in the afternoon.

- Bring out a grab bag containing objects which are pronounced with a short vowel sound. I have included items such as a small doll, a doll's dress, a pen, a small toy sled, and a toy dog. With closed eyes, a child takes something from the bag and then has to say what it is, as well as which vowel is in its name. In a whole-class setting, you'll need to draw a picture on the board so that all the children can see the object associated with the sound. During reading group time, you can just display the objects.

The consonant games described on page 51 can also be adapted to vowels and your students' current needs. For instance, if a reading group has only learned the short *a* and short *i* sounds, just use words containing those sounds on the fish when playing Let's Go Fishing. And, because you want your students to feel successful, you want to make sure they are capable of decoding most of the words on the fish. Here are two additional games you can use with vowels:

- *Bingo* - You can make your own game using either short or long vowels, or sight words.

- *Dolch Group Word Teaching Game* - This commercial game uses a Bingo format to help students recognize basic sight words.

Read! Read! Read!

This is the second part of the integrated approach to reading instruction that I have found successful with a wide range of students. Reading and being read to provide a supportive context for phonics instruction, as well as helping your students become committed and proficient readers.

Children enjoy having books read to them both before they learn to read by themselves and after. Unfortunately, because of television, video games, and our changing lifestyles, many young children aren't being read to at home on a regular basis. This makes your reading aloud every day even more of a necessity. In addition to providing direct support for your reading instruction, it also provides an opportunity for you to act as a role model and transmit your love of books and reading to your students. When you and your students enjoy a story together, you have created a positive learning environment and shared a special moment that will strengthen the bonds between you all. Reading aloud like this also stimulates children's imaginations and opens up new worlds for them. In addition, as they learn that the printed word can entertain as well as inform, they want to hear more stories and are encouraged to read by themselves.

This can be specially important for children who have difficulty learning to read. Max, a 7-year-old with dyslexia and ADHD, had a true love of books but had very few stories read to him at home, because both his parents were so busy with work. Knowing that I would read a book to him each time I saw him, he would always ask at the beginning of a session, "What book are we going to read today?" Then, no matter how restless he was, he made a conscious effort to attend to all our work, so that he would be able to hear a story at the end of the session. He desperately wanted to read and finally did succeed in learning to do so.

Starting with short, simple books helps first graders grow used to sitting and concentrating for an extended period of time, which they may normally do only in front of a television set. That's why I usually begin the year with brief, exciting stories that can be read in one or two sessions. *The Lion and the Mouse* and *Flat Stanley* are two particular favorites early in the year. These stories are so imaginative that children like to have them read again and again.

As the year progresses and the children show that they can attend to simple books, I begin reading short chapter books, such as *Freckle Juice* and others listed in the Resource Section. Most first graders want to hear these books, and because they think the books are very "grown-up," they are proud to be allowed to listen to them. Later, you can start reading longer chapter books, which not only continue to develop students' love of reading, but also help them increase their attention spans.

After I finish reading a story or chapter, we discuss it as a group. I try to elicit children's opinions about the plot, the characters, and what they think might happen next. Besides developing a love of reading, this type of informal class discussion helps develop students' vo-cabulary and language skills. A discussion about unfamiliar words, which we might make a list of, helps children start to familiarize themselves with those words. And, by patterning your language, children learn to discuss what they have heard.

Along with books, other reading material can capture students' interest, as well as support discussions about what they have read. I recently brought in a newspaper article about a famous circus that was coming to town. My first graders were very interested in the topic and enjoyed hearing me read it. I told them about a circus I went to with my family when I was a child, and they told me about their experiences. Then, we talked about what we might find if we went to see the circus described in the article. The possibilities for extending such a discussion are endless. And, you can easily turn this into a reading project, a writing project, an art project, or a combination of all three.

As to reading by themselves, I encourage the students to try as soon as they have learned a few phonic rules and some basic sight words. It's very important that first graders get into the habit of reading, as they will need lots of practice reading aloud in order to become proficient readers. Fortunately, even at this very elementary level, there are a number of books children enjoy reading, such as *Little Bear* and others listed in the Resource Section.

Once your students become more skilled readers, more books become available to them, and you can introduce books about topics of particular interest to individual students. These books can also be used to link reading and writing skills. For example, Jason was a first grader who loved zoos and books that told about zoos or took place in them. Fortunately, I could find these sorts of books at his reading level, and he enjoyed these books so much that he would take them home to read to his younger sister. Then, when I suggested that he write a story about a zoo, he wrote a wonderful story and illustrated it with great care. In this sort of situation, fluent reading and writing can become mutually supportive.

As your students' reading skills improve, suggest a variety of books and give the students a chance to look through them. But first, it's a good idea to talk about the various types of books you are showing them. Often, first grade is the first time children look through books on their own. Some students may not choose to read what you suggest, but others will, and all of them will learn about the wide range of books available to them.

Having worked in many schools, I realize that teachers often have a set reading curriculum they are expected to teach. The approach I am presenting here can be integrated with your school's reading program in various ways, such as using sight words from your required program as your weekly sight words.

Story Notebooks and Other Writing Activities

A Story Notebook is a particularly effective tool for developing students' writing. As mentioned in the preceding chapter, reading specialists need to focus on writing, as well as reading, because these two subjects are so closely intertwined and mutually supportive. Especially in first grade, students need to start to develop the organizational and other techniques that will help them with both types of work.

The Story Notebook contains the set of stories that each child writes during the school year. It may be an actual notebook that can be personalized in various ways, such as having each child decorate his or her own notebook, or letting students choose pieces of material or wallpaper to use as covers. Or, it may be a set of sheets that are kept in folders (which the children write their names on and decorate) until the time is right to bind them together.

For the first few months of school, you will usually need to provide the beginning of each story. With a notebook, that means writing in each child's, a task made much easier when parent volunteers, an aide, or older students can do some of the work. When you're using separate sheets, the "story starter" can be at the top of a sheet, which is then photocopied and handed out with a separate blank sheet for illustrations. Following are some story starters that my first grade students have enjoyed writing about and then illustrating:

- I was on my school bus. It started to fly so...

- I made my street cleaner by...

- As Sam was sitting in his room, his dog Max started talking to him. Max said that...

- One day I was playing baseball. I hit the ball. It broke our window. I was very scared, so...

As the year progresses, you can split the children into pairs, and the child for whom writing is easier can help his or her partner copy a story starter written on the chalkboard. By spring, many of the children may be able to copy from the chalkboard. Of course, first graders need to write about a variety of topics, some of which should be their own ideas. Helping them come up with good ideas may require a lot of additional assistance, but I believe it easier for children to learn to write both about assigned topics and their own ideas at an early age. They should also learn to do imaginative assignments and those that draw on reasoning skills, as well as others in which they describe everyday experiences and must therefore organize information about their lives and put it in sequence. These are all important types of writing that help children develop valuable skills.

In *The Art Of Teaching Writing*, Lucy Calkins suggests providing each child with a separate notebook for ideas. In addition to writing, students can draw pictures on the pages and paste or tape special things brought in from home. When the time comes for students to write stories on their own, they can look through these notebooks for ideas.

In order for your first graders to communicate their ideas in writing effectively, these young students need to learn about capitalization and punctuation. I do this early in the year by introducing the idea that a sentence begins with a capital letter and ends with a period or question mark. As part of this whole class lesson, I write examples of capital letters and punctuation marks on the chalkboard. Then, I write a sentence on the board and ask for a student volunteer to tell us what is needed at the beginning and the end of the sentence.

These lessons continue throughout the year. Sometimes, I will not capitalize the first letter of a sentence and then ask the students if anything is wrong with it. Later in the year, I introduce the exclamation mark, which many children love to use. And, when I review a child's story, I point out where a capital letter or punctuation mark is needed. (It has been my experience that most children like to show that they know about capitalization and punctuation. I believe it is a sign to them that they are "grown up.")

Initially, many students will need a lot of help and encouragement in order to complete a short story, so you must be able to supervise them. This can be done during reading group time or as a whole-class activity. As your students develop their writing skills and become more familiar with the routine, they will be able to work with less supervision in small groups, with a partner, or individually.

Although the amount of supervision the students need decreases over time, you still must recognize the importance of each story a child completes. This can be done by making a personal comment about the story, or writing a supportive note on the page. Some children who love stickers enjoy receiving one and then putting it on the same page with the story they've just written.

I like to have a special "writers' breakfast" with my students a few times each year. Either I bring in some breakfast treats, or I ask parent volunteers to provide them. (One of my colleagues brings in Dunkin' Donuts, which the students find thrilling.) After breakfast, a few of the children get to read their favorite story, and their classmates can ask them questions about it. Of course, this can also be done as a writers' lunch or authors' tea, and inviting the writers' parents to attend can make this an extra-special event.

As educators, an important part of our job is to make sure children realize how special and important their writing is. Even when your students' stories all have the same beginning, the stories and the notebooks that contain them end up being unique.

Language Development

Many children no longer receive adequate opportunities to develop their language skills, and that makes learning to read a far more difficult task. We therefore need to use a variety of methods to help expand first graders' knowledge of and facility with words.

Once a first grader develops these language skills, his or her speaking vocabulary and general verbal fluency can change dramatically for the better. I'll never forget Joe, a kind-hearted and bright but very language-impaired 7-year-old. I knew tremendous progress was occurring when I made my usual Monday inquiry about his weekend, and instead of just saying his usual "good," he started to tell me about the movie he saw and the restaurant where he ate.

With our help and encouragement, children can transfer this sort of new-found ease with language to their writing. A more varied vocabulary begins to appear on the page, and so does a more advanced sentence structure. When a teacher praises a child for these important accomplishments, the child feels enormous pride in his or her work as a student, as well as in the work being done with the teacher. This leads to more self-confidence and often to an increased interest in school work.

In the next few pages, I describe activities that can help first graders develop their language skills. These exercises can be done in your classroom at any time of the day, because students usually enjoy the exercises and do not feel threatened by them. The students can do them as whole-class activities or during reading-group time, and they can be supervised by parent volunteers or mature, older students. In time, your students can also do them independently.

Word Retrieval

You can introduce word retrieval exercises as soon as the school year begins. They are a good way to start because first graders usually think they are easy and fun. Yet, supplying a needed word develops and reinforces the most basic of language skills.

At first, you can just ask students to say a word needed to complete a sentence. An early example would be, "We move the __." Obviously, many words are appropriate answers, but then the sentences can become more specific, such as "I want a football for my __," or "We hit the __."

The next step is to write the sentences on the chalkboard and ask the class what words to fill in. Soon thereafter, you progress to saying and then writing on the board just a few related words—such as *ankle, foot, arm*—instead of a sentence. You ask the students for other words that "go with" these words, and in doing so introduce the concept of categories.

Categorization

Categorization—or listing—makes children think about the way certain objects are related to one another. This skill should be introduced early in the school year—but after you have spent a few sessions practicing word retrieval, because listing related words also serves as a word retrieval exercise.

Ways to practice this skill can range from naming things in students' lives (i.e., things at the playground) to more complex categories (i.e., things that are soft to touch). This makes it an appropriate skill for the entire first grade year, as the categories can change along with the language levels of your students. Usually, first graders enjoy this type of work and are proud when they can think of a number of related words.

You can work on categorization with your class at almost any time during the school day. In addition to asking students to name appropriate words which you then write on a chalk-board or chart, categorization can also be just a verbal activity done in a more spontaneous way. For example, if you have a few extra minutes just before lunch or some other scheduled event, you can announce a category and then ask for volunteers to name a few appropriate items.

Another way to develop these skills is by turning the activities into a five-minute game. Simply divide your class into two or three teams, with a point awarded to each team whenever a member supplies an appropriate word. Deciding on a time limit before the game starts can increase the pressure, which many children seem to enjoy.

At a more advanced level, you can write or say three or four words, and then class members decide which words can be grouped in a category, as well as why the other words do not belong. For example, you might say *car, boat,* and *chair,* and then ask for volunteers who can identify the words that go together, name the category they should be in, and explain why the third word doesn't fit. Of course, this type of activity can also be made more complex over time, and turned into a game by creating teams, awarding points, and imposing time limits.

Similarities And Differences

As part of the language development process, first graders also need to learn how to ex-plain the relationship between objects by discussing their similarities and differences. Initially, this is often a difficult task for children, because they are not used to thinking in this way, so some practice of word retrieval and categorization should come first. Once children start to develop this language skill, they not only tend to be pleased with themselves, their language becomes more expressive.

I find it best to start with simple relationships such as *earrings/necklace* and *orange/grape-fruit.* Bringing in real objects for comparison can also be very helpful. You can then discuss with your students all the ways the items can be alike or different—size, shape, color, texture, etc.

Your students can continue to learn and practice this skill by playing the Similarities/ Differences game. The children are split into two teams, and the members of one team must identify the similarities between two objects. The members of the other team must list the dif-ferences. You can either call on individual members of each team, or have teammates work together to furnish the answers.

Part/Whole Relationships

Recognizing the relationship of parts to a whole is a very important concept, which also teaches first graders some essential vocabulary words. I recommend introducing this concept to first graders early in the school year, either as a whole class or reading group activity.

As with other aspects of language development, the use of real objects helps to introduce a concept and capture students' attention. For example, I have held up a jacket and asked my students to identify the parts. You can also show pictures of objects and then go through a similar process. I keep a collection of pictures of standard items and review them with the students periodically, and I always find it helpful to list the parts on the chalkboard as I discuss them, so children can see as well as hear the answers.

The value of this activity quickly becomes apparent. When I first started doing it, I was surprised at how many first graders did not know the names of important parts of a bicycle, even though many students owned their own bicycles. This same sort of realization helps motivate students and gets them in the habit of learning more detailed names for things.

Another interesting lesson is to ask first graders to look at their hands and name the parts. This can become quite complex, providing an opportunity to introduce many new vocabulary words. I also do the same thing with feet, and I'm frequently amazed at how many first graders do not know words like *ankle* or *heel*.

As students' abilities increase, you can introduce a change by naming parts and asking your students to identify the whole (*nose, wing, engine* or *flowers, trees, benches*). And, throughout the year, these types of exercises can be used to help students keep learning important new words.

Antonyms

In my experience, children enjoy identifying the opposite of a word, so they find working with antonyms fun and usually learn antonyms quickly, which certainly helps expand their vocabulary. When first introducing antonyms to the class, focus on just a few pairs. Then, say one of the words you have just discussed and ask a volunteer to tell the class its opposite. Once children grasp this concept, it is another skill that can be practiced by writing words on the chalkboard—or simply saying a word when children have a few extra minutes—and asking for its opposite. Excellent resources containing word lists and their antonyms include *Language Remediation and Expansion, 150 Skill-Building Reference Lists*, and *HELP—Handbook of Exercises for Language Processing, Volume 2*.

There are also a number of games that can help you teach first graders about antonyms. In Antonym Baseball, you say a word (the pitch) and a students gets a point by saying the opposite word and using it in a sentence. The class can be divided into two teams, or each child can play individually.

Another popular game is Antonym Basketball. For this, you put three wastepaper baskets in the front of the room, designate a few different spots to shoot from, and divide your class into two teams. When you say a word and a child supplies the antonym, using it correctly in a sentence, he or she gets to try to shoot a small, soft ball into one of the baskets. Each basket is worth a certain number of points, depending on the distance from the basket, and because children can get quite involved in this game, setting a time limit in advance is a good idea.

A card game called Antonym Pairs is also an excellent way of learning antonyms. In this matching game, children form word pairs based on words displayed on the cards. This game can be played during reading group time or at some other time, and the Resource Section contains directions for creating the cards.

Once your first graders have had some practice with antonyms, you can write some words on the chalkboard and ask your students to tell you the opposite words, which you write next to the first set of words. Then, you and your students can use these antonym pairs to write a story together, which often becomes quite silly. Next, you read the story to the class and then ask a student volunteer to read it. This popular activity helps your students understand how they can use the words in their everyday language and in their writing.

Developing Auditory Skills

Unfortunately, children's auditory skills have also fallen victims to changes in our lifestyles. A first grader who has already spent countless hours watching television and playing video games—and who continues to do so—is not developing important listening skills that support language development. And, when parents or caregivers do not have or take the time to read aloud to children, this also has a negative impact on students' ability to listen and to read.

Fortunately, educators can help children strengthen their auditory skills by providing opportunities to listen to words and stories in the classroom. This process should start with single words, as first graders learn how to identify the initial, final, and middle sounds of a word (in that order). Usually, children find it easy to hear the beginning and ending sounds of a word, but the middle sounds prove more difficult.

You can start the process by asking questions such as, "Do you hear the *t* sound at the beginning of *time*?" Once children can do this, you can increase the difficulty of the questions by asking, "What sound do you hear at the beginning of the word, *time*?" This same process can be used with the ending and middle sounds, and you can also read a list of six or eight words and ask the children to raise their hands if they hear a particular sounds in the beginning, ending, or middle of a word.

At the same time that you are doing these exercises, you can also begin focusing your students' attention on sound blending. The best way to start is with two-phoneme words (*ch-ew, g-o, t-oy*) and then move to three- and four-phoneme words (*h-ea-d* and *f-i-ng-er*). At the beginning of first grade, in particular, four-phoneme words are likely to be too difficult.

In addition to practicing these skills, you should also make sure all your students have or develop sufficient rhyming skills—especially the children who showed weakness on the rhyming section of the reading evaluation. Although rhyming skills were probably taught in kindergarten, some first graders continue to have great difficulty with identifying and completing rhymes. To strengthen this skill, you can give your students three words (*fun, fin, run,*) and ask which two rhyme. Another way is to read an incomplete sentence (I like to ride my_____.), stressing the key word *like*, and ask students to complete it with a word that rhymes

The book, *Language Remediation & Expansion—150 Skill Building Reference Lists*, is an excellent resource for this type of exercise, which can just be practiced for short periods of time. As with the other exercises described in this section, ten minutes a few times a week is usually sufficient.

In addition to developing first graders' auditory discrimination, you also need to help them strengthen their auditory memory, including both words and events. Children usually enjoy doing this type of work if you go slowly and use exercises that are set up for success. For example, you can say, "Let's see how many words you can remember. Listen carefully, and when I am done, I will ask you to tell me the words that I said." Start with three words in a category (*cake, ice cream, Jell-O*), and when your students can remember related words, you can start using unrelated words (*pig, door, desk*). Slowly, you determine whether they can remember four words or perhaps even five. *Help 1—Handbook of Exercises for Language Processing* is a fine source for this type of material.

You also want to help your students strengthen their recall of stories and information. Obviously, your daily story time is very important in this regard. In addition, I would recommend that you read paragraphs to your class at other times and ask them questions about what you have just read. You can use paragraphs from children's magazines, a weekly reader, or a simple book likely to be of interest to your students. This sort of work can be done with a whole class or in small groups.

By combining this sort of emphasis on language skills development with intensive work on reading and writing, you will be providing your first graders with the solid foundation they need to read, write, and succeed in the years ahead.

CHAPTER 4

Becoming A Second Grade Reading Specialist

Second grade is always a fascinating year, filled with diversity and change. Children start the year with a wide range of abilities and skills, which they then consolidate, improve, and make automatic. Some children who were still struggling to decode short words in September become able readers, and their pride in this accomplishment is clear. Others start by reading simple stories and soon turn into fluent readers who are engrossed in chapter books.

For many, writing also becomes a less onerous task. Some students still have trouble with letter formation at the beginning of the year, and for others constructing a simple sentence is a frustrating experience that results in numerous erasures and crossed out words. With continued instruction and support, however, many students find that encoding is no longer a tremendous effort that requires a great deal of time. Their letters are clearly formed, their handwriting flows, and writing a story is an enjoyable and satisfying project.

Often, the children become more interested in different facets of language. Words start to intrigue them, and in particular second graders love to hear about "sound alike" words. When you tell them that these words are called *homophones* and write that word on the board, the children are very impressed.

Second graders also delight in telling jokes that are "a play on words." This is the year of the joke book, and stories based on misperceptions of words are also popular. *Amelia Bedelia* is a perennial second grade favorite.

As their sophistication and independence increases, second graders want the types of books they read to expand. They want to learn factual information about people, geography, and history. And, they like stories about characters who are experiencing independence, too, such as *Pippi Longstocking* and *The Box Car Children*. Also popular are child detectives who are in control of their world and can solve mysteries, like those found in *Nate the Great* and *The Pizza Monster*, .

Of course, second graders are not as self-reliant and grown-up as they sometimes would like us to believe. If you poll them (a favorite second grade activity), you're likely to find that many still believe in Santa Claus and the Tooth Fairy. They still need to play, build, and exercise at school, and many are going through big physical, emotional, and intellectual changes. This can be scary, so second graders often welcome our limits and rules. At a time when more and more is expected of them, knowing the rules provides security, which is why children of this age are so serious about "sticking to the rules" when playing kickball or other games.

For the second grade teacher, this is the year when many students start to "get" the skills and concepts their first grade teachers were trying to help them learn. Second grade teachers develop and build on the reading, writing, and language skills introduced in first grade, teaching important new skills as the students become ready. The rationale for teaching this way is simple. Not all children are at the same level at the same time in the same area, so the students' individual learning profiles have to be kept in mind.

The "game plan" for second grade includes more comprehension skills and an expansion of the writing program. Most second graders can comprehend what they read, if they can decode it, so we must make sure that the basic decoding skills learned in first grade are secure and automatic. Some students will need several months to review the phonics skills and sight words originally taught in first grade. Once this is done, you can introduce more word recognition and decoding skills. However, the "problem readers" in second grade are children who cannot yet break the reading code, and they need heavy doses of decoding and/or word recognition work.

Oral reading is also stressed in second grade, because it helps students become fluent readers. When they read aloud, second graders learn the importance of word analysis and phonics, and they start to learn effective oral reading strategies. In addition, as second grade progresses, children spend more time reading silently, using interesting and appropriate materials to practice word recognition and decoding skills they have learned. Second grade is also when students start to learn how to obtain information from a text, and the combination of all these different reading experiences helps them become accurate, independent readers.

Other important parts of the reading and language development program started in first grade are continued and expanded in second grade. Reading is emphasized throughout the school day, as are writing, language, and auditory skills. One new step is the introduction of an organized spelling program.

My overall strategy for carrying out this approach remains the same as in first and in third grade:

1. Evaluate your students' skills and abilities, and use this information as the basis for forming your reading groups.

2. Implement an organized, sequential learning program.

3. Teach your students to work independently as well as in groups.

4. Use an integrated approach that combines phonics and whole language techniques.

Evaluating Second Graders' Reading

The Informal Reading Evaluation included in this chapter is an effective diagnostic tool that provides a lot of pertinent information you need about your students' reading. It is easy to administer and interpret, and it gives you a good sense of each child's general knowledge, grapho-motor skills, reading readiness, and reading skills. This evaluation includes some general questions, a handwriting sample, and short assessments that reveal students' knowledge of the alphabet, phonics, and sight words, as well as their rhyming and oral reading skills.

I recommend administering this evaluation during the first few weeks of school. You need to pick the best time of day to take students aside individually (I prefer doing this when the class is doing assigned "seat work" or involved in quiet play.), and have the chart that lists your students' names alongside columns corresponding to the variety of assessments you'll be administering.

Before beginning the evaluation, I make sure to tell each child that this work will help me to see what he or she learned in first grade, so that I will then know what to teach in second grade. I add that I do not expect anyone to know everything I ask (because this helps to relieve children's anxiety about their performance). During the evaluation, I praise the child's efforts and might provide encouragement by saying, "That's a good answer," or "You almost have it. Look at it again." This type of comment can help keep a child feeling involved and at ease, so that you then obtain an optimal performance.

The general information questions are a good way to start the evaluation, because second graders usually do not find these questions threatening. And, your students' answers can reveal quite a lot about them.

When children tell you their birthdays, do they mention the year they were born? Very few second graders do this. When you ask for the name of the current month, you'll find out whether each child can remember and retrieve information that you probably mention every day as part of the "morning meeting." And, when you ask what the hottest months are, you'll

Second Grade Reading Evaluation
For durability I suggest that you mount the different parts of the test on large index cards.

Naming Lower Case Letters

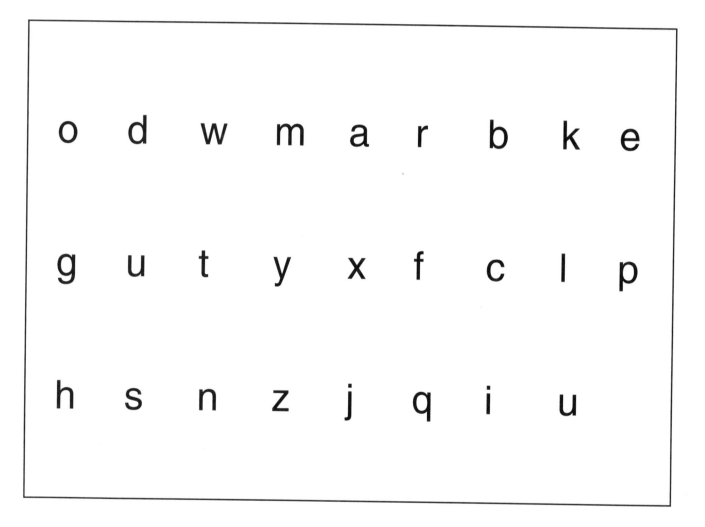

Saying Letter Sounds

c d n f s t p

b l k r x j y

w m q h v g z

Nonsense Words

Tests 5-7

rab	ped	vin	mog	lub
bave	mede	lipe	sobe	tule
preal	sloam	stail	smeef	
tway	skoe			

Sight Words

funny   four   pretty   want   could

every   there   after   once   who

Second Grade Oral Reading Test - Student Passage Sheet

Mom and I live in a big city.
One day we go for a walk.
We see many cars on the street.
"I like the red car," says Mom.
"I like the pretty blue car," I say.
We see boys and girls playing.
They play ball in a small lot.

I help my mother and father.
I work in the house.
When my little sister cries I play with her.
Then she laughs.
I walk our big black dog Spot.
I go to the store for milk.
One day I helped my Dad.
I cut the grass and helped Dad cut down a tree.

When my sister had her birthday Mom and Dad bought her a puppy. What a puppy it was! Sometimes my sister would let me play with the puppy. I dreamed about it! How I wanted one of my own.

Then on my birthday they bought me one, too. They even gave me a dish and a toy for the puppy. It was the happiest day.

Williamsburg is a very famous city in Virginia. People from all over go there to see it.

Much of Williamsburg has been made to look just as it did in the 1700s, when it was the capital of the state. Some buildings that had burned down have been rebuilt. Men and women dressed in clothes like those worn in the 1700s welcome the visitors. They tell how people lived and worked in those early times.

Reprinted by permission of Educators Publishing Service.

Karl Wallenda was the most famous high-wire walker in circus history. Sadly, he was killed in 1978. While he was walking on a 75 foot cable strung between two buildings, a gust of wind made him lose his balance.

Karl was born into a circus family in Germany in 1905. His father was a catcher in a flying trapeze act. As children Karl and his brother performed acrobatic stunts in front of restaurants, and people threw money in a hat for them.

While he was still a boy, he joined a high-wire act. At seventeen he was so good that he had his own act.

Reprinted by permission of Educators Publishing Service.

Second Grade Informal Test - Student Record Sheet

Student's Name: _____

Date: _____

Date of Birth: _____

I. General Information

1. When is your birthday? _____

2. What month is this? _____

3. Where is the best place to borrow a book? _____

4. What is one of the hottest months of the year? _____

5. What day comes before Wednesday? _____

6. What month comes after March? _____

II. Handwriting Sample:

Teacher Comments:

III. Informal Reading Skills Test

1. Naming Lower Case Letters

   Letters Missed: _____

   Number Correct: _____

2. Giving Letter Sounds

   Letters Missed: _____

   Number Correct: _____

3. Rhyming
   Sample: What word rhymes with Dad? If the student cannot think of a word, supply one.

Tell me a word that rhymes with

   hat   _____

   bake   _____

   jail   _____

   heat   _____

   lamp   _____

   lid   _____

   Number Correct: _____

4. Sound Blending
   Pronounce as shown in first column. Have the student try again, if the first response is incorrect. Note both answers. Give full credit, if the second attempt is correct.

   1. s-o   (so)   _____

   2. sh-oe   (shoe)   _____

   3. ch-arm   (charm)   _____

   4. t-oo-th   (tooth)   _____

   5. m-i-l-k   (milk)   _____

   6. p-e-pp-er   (pepper)   _____

   Number Correct: _____

5. Short Vowel Words

1. rab   _____

2. ped   _____

3. vin   _____

4. mog   _____

5. lub   _____

Number Correct: _____

6. The Magic e Words

1. bave   _____

2. mede   _____

3. lipe   _____

4. sobe   _____

5. tule   _____

Number Correct: _____

7. Two Vowels Together Words

1. preal   _____

2. sloam   _____

3. stail   _____

4. smeef   _____

5. tway   _____

6. skoe   _____

Number Correct: _____

8. Sight Words

1. funny   _____
2. four   _____
3. pretty   _____
4. want   _____
5. could   _____
6. every   _____
7. there   _____
8. after   _____
9. once   _____
10. who   _____

Number Correct: _____

IV. The Oral Reading Test And Checklist

Primer

Mom and I live in a big city.
One day we go for a walk.
We see many cars on the street.
"I like the red car," says Mom.
"I like the pretty blue car," I say.
We see boys and girls playing.
They play ball in a small lot.

Errors: _____

Grade 1

I help my mother and father.

I work in the house.

When my little sister cries I play with her.

Then she laughs.

I walk our big black dog Spot.

I go to the store for milk.

One day I helped my Dad.

I cut the grass and helped Dad cut down a tree.

Errors: _____

Grade 2

When my sister had her birthday Mom and Dad bought her a puppy. What a puppy it was! Sometimes my sister would let me play with the puppy. I dreamed about it! How I wanted one of my own.

Then on my birthday they bought me one, too. They even gave me a dish and a toy for the puppy. It was the happiest day.

Errors: _____

Grade 3

Williamsburg is a very famous city in Virginia. People from all over go there to see it.

Much of Williamsburg has been made to look just as it did in the 1700s, when it was the capital of the state. Some buildings that had burned down have been rebuilt. Men and women dressed in clothes like those worn in the 1700s welcome the visitors. They tell how people lived and worked in those early times.

Reprinted by permission of Educators Publishing Service.

Errors: _____

Grade 4

Karl Wallenda was the most famous high-wire walker in circus history. Sadly, he was killed in 1978. While he was walking on a 75 foot cable strung between two buildings, a gust of wind made him lose his balance.

Karl was born into a circus family in Germany in 1905. His father was a catcher in a flying trapeze act. As children Karl and his brother performed acrobatic stunts in front of restaurants, and people threw money in a hat for them.

While he was still a boy, he joined a high-wire act. At seventeen he was so good that he had his own act.

Reprinted by permission of Educators Publishing Service.

Errors: _____

Checklist of Type of Errors Made

_____ mispronunciations

_____ hesitations

_____ repetitions

_____ omissions

_____ additions

Additional comments:

Approximate Oral Reading Level: _____

find that most students know summer is hot, but naming specific months requires an even better memory and retrieval ability. Asking what month comes after March, as well as what day comes before Wednesday, requires a child to sequence information in addition to remembering and retrieving it.

Asking where a good place to borrow a book would be helps you check on a child's common sense and experience. It can also help you determine whether or how often a child goes to the local library and reads with his or her family.

Next, you ask the student to write his or her name and address on a piece of paper. If the student only writes a first name, ask if he or she can write the last name or any of the letters in it. Many second graders still have difficulty writing their complete last name and address, as this requires a good visual memory. Also be sure to note how each student holds the pencil. An incorrect pencil grip should be noted on the Student Record Sheet.

Meanwhile, the way the child writes gives you a general idea of his or her grapho-motor skills. Most second graders print their name and address, but some try to write in script. You can also see whether the letters are formed correctly, there is adequate spacing between words, and the writing is fluid. Comparing a few students' writing samples can give you a good perspective on these factors.

The next phase of the evaluation is comprised of three sub-tests that assess skills usually covered thoroughly in kindergarten. First, the child is asked to identify all the lower-case letters, which should be automatic by second grade. If not, you know the child is "at risk" and probably needs more extensive evaluation, as well as intensive instruction and support. Next, the student is asked to say the sounds made by all the consonants. If a child hesitates, provide a moment for the child to think, and if there's still no response, move on to the next letter. I would expect second graders to know the sound associated with each letter. Those who do not know these sound/symbol relationships need direct instruction and practice, so they can successfully blend sounds together to make words while reading.

The rhyming test checks a student's ability to come up with words that sound similar— a key aspect of learning phonics. I start with a sample question, such as "What word rhymes with Dad?", and if the child cannot think of a word, I provide an example. Then, I ask the student to say a word that rhymes with each of the six test words. A child who can do five out of six is demonstrating mastery, while a child who can do none or very few is likely to have difficulty working with "word families" and other key aspects of phonics.

After the rhyming test come four sub-tests that cover other skills that are standard first grade fare. The first sub-test in this section evaluates how well a child can blend the parts of a word together, after you say the parts slowly. I give a child full credit if he or she can say the word correctly on a second try, and I would consider saying five out of six words correctly a demonstration of mastery. Blending is a very important element of an early reading program, and if a child does poorly at this, additional blending work (see page 116) should be part of the child's program.

In each of the following three sub-tests, the student is asked to decode nonsense words, which are used to prevent the child from using his or her sight vocabulary. In this way, you can determine whether the child has learned and can apply some basic phonic skills. These sub-tests cover short-vowel words, magic *e* words, and two-vowels-together words. I would consider saying 4 out of 5 in each category correctly to be a demonstration of mastery. If a child cannot pronounce at least one of the first three words correctly, I go on to the next category, because there is no point in frustrating the child, who has already revealed that he or she needs help with the entire category of words.

You should make sure to note which words are not pronounced correctly, as this tells you which types of skills are unknown and need to be taught. For example, if a child says "real" instead of "preal," that shows the child knows the two-vowels-together rule, but not the *pr* blend. Also note how the student "attacks" a word. Is there an attempt to sound out a word, or does the child rely on sight memory?

An additional sub-test reveals whether a child can recognize and pronounce some basic sight words. I would consider saying nine out of ten correctly to be a passing grade. If a child knows many of the sight words but had trouble with the nonsense words, he or she may be a natural sight reader—or perhaps phonics was not taught in the child's first grade classroom. That's why at this point I like to ask a few quick questions about how the child learned to read, which can reveal a great deal of information.

The Oral Reading Test shows how well a second grader can use his or her decoding skills and sight vocabulary while reading aloud. Generally, I recommend that you begin with the first grade passage, but if a child had marked difficulty with the skills evaluation, start with the "primer" passage. As the student reads the material from the Student Passage Sheet, you follow along using the Oral Reading Record Sheet and noting errors above the specific words, in addition to jotting down any impressions.

There are some mistakes that I do not count as errors. If a child mispronounces a proper name, for example, or leaves off an *s* at the end of a word, or says "a" instead of "the," I would disregard the mistake because it is a common one that does not affect the meaning of the text.

However, as soon as a student makes five or more of the following errors during the reading of a passage, you should stop the Oral Reading Test, because the passage is too difficult and the child has reached his or her limit. You already have a good idea of the child's oral reading ability, and there is no point in frustrating the child.

Here are the types of errors that should be counted:

Mispronunciations - If a student mispronounces a word (other than a proper name) or part of a word, be sure to note it and write the child's pronunciation phonetically. An example would be when a child says *chip* for *trip* or *his* for *had*.

Reversals - If a student reverses the order of letters in a word, write down the reversal. Common examples are *was* for *saw* and *pan* for *nap*.

Hesitations - If a student hesitates for more than five seconds, say the word. Also say the word when a student says he or she does not know the word. Then, draw a line through the text.

Repetitions - If a student repeats two or more words, I count this as an error unless the child is correcting a previous error, as the goals in this part of the evaluation are accuracy and fluency.

Omissions - If a student leaves out a whole word or part of a word (other than an *s* at the end), this is counted as an error. Draw a circle around the omitted word or word part.

Additions - If a student inserts a word or word part that does not actually appear in the passage, I count this as an error. Write the added word or word part above a caret (^).

Once a child has completed the Oral Reading Test, thank the child for his or her work, and then use the Checklist of Types of Errors (found on the Student Record Sheet) to note the type of errors made and jot down any final impressions. Did the student disregard punctuation, read too rapidly or slowly, read word-by-word, or give up too quickly?

This combination of errors and impressions is the basis for your estimation of the child's oral reading level. I believe, as do many other reading specialists, that five errors or more indicate a passage is too difficult. A passage in which a child makes fewer than three errors indicates his independent reading level, while three or four errors indicate the appropriate instructional level.

After completing your evaluation of the first few students, you're also likely to notice some typical behavior patterns. Usually, second graders are quite willing to answer the general information questions and write their names and addresses. Some students will have difficulty writing their complete address, and the worriers among them will say, "I don't know my whole address." However, at this point in the evaluation very few second graders are very concerned if they don't know something.

As the evaluation becomes more challenging, though, the reactions become more varied. Some second graders are pluggers and continue trying very hard. Some just say quietly, "I don't know," or "I haven't learned this." Others lose their concentration when the work becomes challenging and are easily distracted, or they start to rush and make wild guesses. These are all typical testing behaviors.

You'll also start to notice some typical learning patterns. A few second graders will have difficulty with some of the first sections of the evaluation, and their difficulties become more apparent as the evaluation progresses. Their performance pattern is weak, so you know these children need a reading program that goes slowly and includes plenty of time for review. Some of these students cannot think of rhyming words, which indicates that the "word family" approach to reading will be difficult for them. Other children have trouble blending word parts together, so they also will need additional help in order to learn phonics.

With your average second grade readers, you will notice other patterns. As they work on the test, you will see that some children have a stronger phonics background than others. These second graders find the nonsense words easier to decode than the sight words, while the reverse is true for second graders who learned to read using the sight word methods. You'll therefore want to utilize each child's strengths while also reinforcing the skills and approach that are not as strong.

Also see if you can discover any patterns in your students' oral reading. Usually, your second graders' oral reading scores will vary widely—probably ranging from primer-level (or below) to third grade or above. In addition to looking at the scores, you should review how individual students tried to decode unknown words. If they tried to sound them out, and did better decoding the nonsense words than the sight words on the reading skills test, they would probably benefit from an emphasis on phonics. Other second graders, who depend on their knowledge of sight words when they read aloud and do better with sight words than nonsense words on the reading skills test, will probably experience more success with a sight word approach initially, but still need to learn phonics so they can decode new words in the future.

Make sure to note any telling comments on the Student Record Sheet. If a child gives an incorrect verbal answer, write down what is said and later consider what type of error it is. Did the child make a wild guess, or was he or she trying to break down the word?

These sorts of insights, combined with the specific test scores, will help you make up your reading groups. Students with similar profiles will benefit from being placed together so that, for example, students who already know the "two-vowels-together" words do not have to sit through the same lessons as children who need to learn or review their short vowel sounds.

You may find that a few children did well on the reading skills test but had difficulty with the oral reading test, or vice versa. In this sort of situation, you must use your own judgment. Make sure to consider whether the children were nervous or distracted during a particular test, as this can have a strong influence on the test score. Obviously, this is not a standardized test, and you need to confirm your initial evaluation as you proceed with your reading assignments, direct instruction, and reading group formation.

The Student Record Sheet and results of this evaluation should remain in the student's file throughout the year, as they provide baseline information about reading skills and abilities at the start of the year. They also can prove very helpful and informative during parent-teacher conferences.

Organizing And Working With Your Reading Groups

The primary purpose of reading groups—and the way in which they should be organized—is the same in second grade as it is in first grade, so rather than repeat that information, I will just refer readers who haven't read Chapter 3 to pages 33-36. The two main advantages of reading groups also remain the same but are probably worth repeating here: working with smaller groups enables you to provide more individualized attention to the group's members, and teaching something to a small group is often more effective and supportive than teaching something to the whole class, because what you teach is relevant to everyone in the group, due to their similar needs and abilities.

I also want to emphasize again that while you should organize reading groups so that the children in them have similar reading skills, these placements should be re-evaluated throughout the year and changed as needed. And, you need to make sure the children understand you are organizing them into these groups just so you can teach them better during the (hour-and-a-half) reading period in the morning.

Second graders tend to be even better suited than first graders to the independent work that is an essential part of the routine when you are working with three reading groups for thirty minutes each. Your students are now likely to have a greater attention span and be better able to handle longer assignments, so they are more self-sufficient. Second graders are also expected to spend more time reading their assigned books, and as the year progresses, they must answer some of their reading comprehension assignments in full sentences and begin to spend more time on various writing projects. While the members of other groups are busy with this sort of work, you can be working intensively with one group.

Of course, you still need to provide different types of reading-related projects for your students to do as independent work, so they don't lose interest. These sorts of projects can include using their own words to write an extension of a story that they read or you read to them, or completing reading comprehension or language development sheets you provide.

Second graders also enjoy using a picture format to re-tell a story they read or you read to them. The first time this is done it should be a class project, so everyone learns what to do.

Explain that they should draw the main events of the story, and have them fold pieces of paper into sixths or eighths. This can be done individually, or with one partner, or as a team. Then, they show their work to the class. Once the process is understood, having two children work together can be particularly effective, if a proficient reader is paired with a child who is a weaker reader but a talented artist.

Knowing that some of your students do not need as much phonics and sight word practice as others, you can have them work more on the basic reading comprehension skills you teach during their reading group time. You can give them practice sheets that provide an interesting story followed by multiple choice or short fill-in questions. Your students need to practice learning how to find the main idea, comprehend the sequence of events, and draw a conclusion. To help them do this, you can use your own and/or commercially prepared materials.

Of course, remembering that the amount of silent reading compared to oral reading should increase as the year progresses, you also want to make sure your students have opportunities to practice reading during their independent reading group time. This should include stories and books they have already read.

While you are working with one reading group, the students working independently can also engage in a variety of other reading-related activities. For example, because learning to write is so closely intertwined with learning to read, this is a good time to practice handwriting or work on other writing projects. Some second graders still need to practice manuscript handwriting while others are experimenting with cursive, so appropriate practice sheets can be included in your students' Learning Packets. Students can also write in their Story Notebook (see page 58), or do pre-paragraph exercises or paragraph writing, or write a story using descriptive words from a story they have read. (Write the descriptive words at the top of the students' papers.) Later, these stories can be shared with the rest of the reading group.

As the year progresses, the students spend longer amounts of time writing during their independent reading group time. At the beginning of the year, though, you have to provide a variety of activities for them to do if they finish a writing assignment early. They can tape a story or some poetry, for example, or write riddles for a riddle book, and these sorts of projects can be done on an individual basis or with a peer.

They can also play educational games which reinforce reading skills by focusing attention on phonic sounds, sight vocabulary words or rules the students are studying. As described in more detail on page 51, Climb and Slide, Shoot to the Stars, Let's Go Fishing, Robert's Treasure, Memory, and Indianapolis 500 are enjoyable games that support the learning process and are easy to make (directions are in the Resource Section).

To vary the routine during reading group time, you can also introduce the following activities:

1. Have a few children write a play about a book they have read, with each child having a turn to do the actual writing. Invite them to present the play to the class, and provide a few simple props to make it more enjoyable and engaging.

2. Ask the children to use their own words to write a story that they read or had read to them. After they write it, have them tape it.

3. Ask a few children to choose and read an article or short story from the classroom library. Once they have finished reading it, they should give their peers an oral summary of what they read. And, when you have a free moment during the day, have them tell you what the article or story is about. This exercise not only encourages silent reading, it teaches children how to summarize. Of course, in order to summarize successfully, they have to understand what they have read, so this is a tried and true way to help develop reading comprehension.

As in first grade, managing your reading groups is much easier when you have access to aides, parent volunteers, or older students who supervise the independent work of the groups you are not working with at any particular time. An effective alternative could be a carefully arranged cooperative learning plan, which can work even better in second grade because you have members of either the middle or advanced reading group who can help members of the "emerging" group.

Creating & Using The Learning Packet

Described in detail in the chapter on Becoming A First Grade Reading Specialist (see pages 37-47), the Learning Packet contains a variety of assignments that your other students work on independently while you are working with a different reading group. This remains an effective tool throughout second grade, and as the year progresses and your students become more proficient in reading, writing, and language work, they become capable of handling a greater variety of assignments. Of course, during the year, you will first need to introduce the information, skills, and types of assignments, either as a whole-class lesson or in individual reading groups.

Once the students grow used to the routine, they should be able to do the Learning Packet assignments on their own. If not, review the assignments and consider whether they are too demanding. I use the same criteria across the grades for evaluating whether assignments are appropriate: your students should be able to get 75 to 80 percent of the work done correctly, most of the time. If this is not happening and the children are applying themselves, the work is too hard. Sometimes, however, a few children may just be having difficulty with a particular concept.

Your students should not be expected to spend too long a time on any one task. I find that when children have a number of different assignments, they stay more involved in their work.

And, knowing that practice sheets provide needed reinforcement but can become boring for students, varying the formats can help "sweeten the medicine."

The Learning Packet should include phonics and language practice sheets, which reinforce specific concepts and skills in various ways. For example, as shown on the accompanying pages, reviewing something like the sounds of *oo* can be done in a few different ways to keep things interesting, while still providing continuity and a sustained focus.

As your students become more proficient readers, you'll want to include more trade books in their Learning Packets, along with reading comprehension work. You can use various reading skill sheets or give your students reading workbooks. I recommend the following series: *Reading About Science, Specific Skill Series, Comprehension We Use,* and *Catching On.* Second graders usually enjoy these materials, which reinforce important reading comprehension skills that you first introduce to a reading group. However, you'll want to preview these materials to see if they're too advanced for the skill levels of some of your groups.

Learning Packets should also contain handwriting practice sheets for those second graders who need them. Most second graders remain concerned about the beauty and neatness of their writing, so I suggest you take advantage of this interest by having them practice and perfect this skill as part of their independent work during reading group time. During the second half of the year, you'll also add a composition book for paragraph writing.

Following are two typical Learning Packet assignments for second graders, who can do them while you are teaching one of the other reading groups. The time of year in which you assign this work depends on the students' reading level. Usually, the first assignment would be introduced in the fall to your advanced and middle groups, but your emerging group may not be able to do this type of work until the winter. The second assignment would usually be introduced in the spring, although some students are not ready to learn diphthongs until third grade. The same formats can be used for other phonic sounds, and the formats can be varied to make the work either more or less challenging, depending on the skill levels of your reading groups.

In the fall, when your students are reviewing or learning the "two-vowels-together" rule, their Learning Packets should contains practice sheets that help them with a number of vowel combinations they have already practiced (*ee, ea, ai, ay, oa*). One sheet might have a set of boxes with three words and a picture in each box, many of the words will be vowel digraphs. The students' assignment is to read the words in each box and circle the word that goes with the picture. The next sheet might have sentences with accompanying pictures. The students have to read three sentences and choose which sentence goes with the accompanying picture. On a third sheet, students would complete a brief story by filling in appropriate vowel digraph words on blank lines embedded in the text.

Say these words. If the <u>oo</u> sounds the way it does in moon, write it under moon. If the <u>oo</u> sounds like it does in book, write it under book.

tool   groom brook   wool   shoot   broom
scoop   shook crook   stood

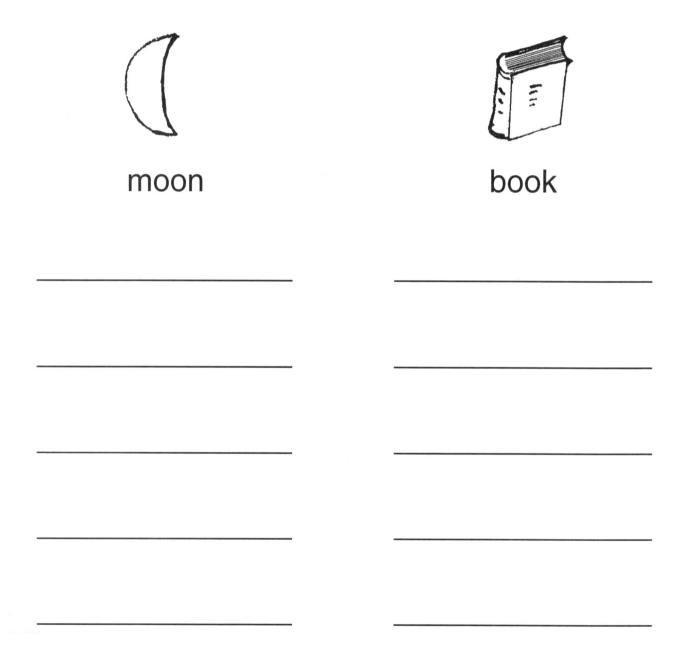

moon   book

_____   _____

_____   _____

_____   _____

_____   _____

_____   _____

All the words that answer these riddles have <u>oo</u> in them. Write the answers in the blanks.

1. What do you hang your coat on? _____

2. What do you eat jello with? _____

3. What do your sweep with? _____

4. What is the top of a house called? _____

5. What time is it at twelve? _____

6. What is a horse's foot called? _____

7. What is the name of the part of

   a plant that is under ground? _____

8. What is another word for a

   small stream? _____

9. What is another word for great? _____

10 Where can you swim? _____

Circle the word that goes with the picture.

leak

leaf

lunch

Jeep

jail

Jean

coat

toast

coast

trade

train

sprain

champ

chain

chess

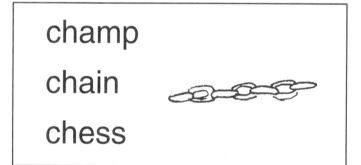

trick

tray

trade

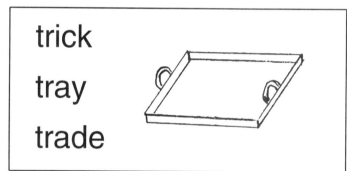

street

fleet

seed

press

pray

pride

rope

road

read

spill

speak

steam

✔ the one that goes with the picture.

1. For a treat the goat eats a grey coat.

   The goat likes to eat soap.

   The sick girl dreams of going to the beach.

2. The meal was so good it was like a feast.

   The boy gets a paint stain on his coat.

   You must pay to take a boat ride.

3. The geese flew to the man with the gun.

   Ray sits on the road to wait for the train.

   Mom's jeep tire needs some more air.

4. The queen has two long braids.

   In Spain Gail plays on the beach all day.

   The beast had a feast on Jean's beans.

5. The boy soaks in the hot tub to get clean.

   The deer eats the weeds and then sleeps all day.

   Moe stayed by the bay all day to play.

✔ the one that goes with the picture.

6. Joe thinks it a treat to eat sweet plums.

   Mom paid me to spray green paint on the mail box.

   Jay went up the tree to reach a peach.

7. The rat dreams of eating a big cheese.

   Steve sweeps the road with a rake.

   Jean eats a big meal at the beach.

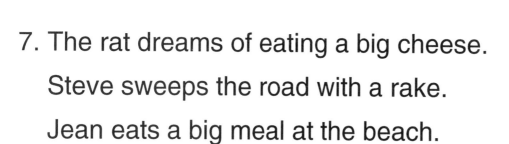

Use these words to complete the story.

pails   beach   train   boats   played
jeep   roast   day   treat

Mom said we could go to the _____. We

had a new _____, and it was a

_____ to ride in it to the beach. On the

way a _____ passed us, and we waved.

At the beach we _____ all _____

with our _____ and _____. Mom

let us _____ hot dogs.

These sorts of practice sheets can come from workbooks, such as those recommended in the Resource Section, or you can create your own. Either way, they can be used with different reading groups at appropriate times, year after year.

In addition, children enjoy creating their own practice sheets, and these can be very effective learning tools. Give each of the students a sample sheet and then ask them to create their own list of six or seven words that have two vowels together in them such as *boat*, *pail*, or *feet*. (They can refer to a list posted in the front of the room if they need ideas.) Have them leave a space next to each word for a picture, and then exchange sheets with their neighbors. After completing the sheets, the students can compare their work with each other.

The Learning Packets should also contain some short phonics books for students to read to themselves, thereby gaining further practice with the two-vowels-together rule. Suitable books for this and other aspects of phonics include *Phonics Practice Readers*, *Primary Phonics*, and *Steck-Vaughn Phonics Readers*.

Another important component would be some simple reading comprehension sheets. I find that children who are just beginning to decode are often so intent on this process, they do not think about what they are reading. To help them develop this skill, I find two exercises particularly helpful. One is to create a sheet of sentences, some of which are silly. (*The purple cow jumped over the can of paint.*) The number and complexity of the sentences should depend on the students' reading proficiency, as their assignment is to circle the ones that are silly. The other exercise is to create a sheet containing only scrambled sentences, along with space for the sentences to be rearranged so they make sense. (*Can jeep a rain go in the?*) When creating this sort of sheet, make sure to start the sentence with the correct first word.

You can also use a variety of short, simple reading comprehension materials from different publishers. However, some of your advanced readers may not need this type of exercise, in which case I suggest that you give them more work in some of the reading workbooks referred to above.

In the spring, a typical Learning Packet assignment would review the vowel digraph *oo*. A practice sheet might provide a list of *oo* words or have students pick 5 or 6 from a longer list written across the top, which each student would then use in a paragraph written on the sheet. Once the students have finished, they can read their paragraphs to each other. (If you think some children will have trouble with this assignment, you can have them work in pairs.) In this way, you are utilizing a creative approach to phonics practice that also supports a number of other aspects of language development. And, once your students grow used to writing paragraphs like this, you can increase the number of specified words they must use.

Next, the students silently read a short phonics book that provides additional practice with the *oo* sound. Then, they can read a book which they have chosen and you have approved, based on their reading proficiency. After finishing the book, each student should explain in writing what the story is about, and you can have each child write about a favorite character.

This is a good time for an aide or parent volunteer to circulate, checking students' work and offering help when it appears needed. If you are using peer helpers, you need to decide whether they should actually correct their classmates' work. Keep in mind how sensitive second graders are. Depending on the students involved, you may decide that helpers can provide information but not put any marks or writing on a sheet.

Knowing that students finish their work at different times and you will be busy working with another reading group, you need to have set routines established (which you briefly review at the start of reading group time) for students who finish their work early. Of course, you may decide that certain children need to work on specific skills, in which case you suggest that they do specific activities. For example, most second graders need practice with oral reading. Rereading a passage or book helps to increase fluency; an effective and enjoyable way for students to do this is taping a chapter or story they read in their reading group. This can be done as an independent project, in pairs, or in small groups.

You can also have your students work on the following two exercises, which help develop reading comprehension as well as writing skills. The first exercise is to have the students use their own words to rewrite a story they read in class or you read to them. Show them how they can illustrate the story by folding a piece of paper into sixths or eighths and sketching an important moment in each box. You can also have your students write comprehension questions for a Weekly Reader story. At first, you should provide supervision and direction for both these activities, which can then be done individually or as a cooperative learning project once the students have more experience.

Another activity is to have your second graders write their own silly sentences using particular sounds they are studying, such as the *oo* sound. You'll want to have a list of *oo* words displayed in the front of the room and on the practice sheets, which will also have a few sample silly word sentences at the top. (Scott was too hot to hoot. Jane has a mushroom tattoo.) The students should use as many of the *oo* words as they can, and you can offer a reward to students who create sentences containing *oo* words that are not on the sheet. This is an excellent project for one student, pairs, or small groups, and the results can be taped or read to the rest of the class.

Phonics & Whole Language
—An Integrated Approach

As noted earlier, I do not believe there is just one, single method that will teach children to read. In second grade, as in the other grades, children need an integrated approach that combines whole language techniques with a strong, systematic phonics program.

A phonics program is the "key" that helps most children "unlock the door" to reading. It works best when you and your students can focus on phonic elements found in words from reading materials and other subject areas, rather than just arbitrary and disconnected examples. In addition, sight words also play an important part in helping all your students become successful readers in second grade, because a fluent reader needs strong phonics skills and a good sight vocabulary. While the evaluations you did at the start of the year will help you determine which students favor a sight word approach and which are phonetic readers, each group also needs to work on the other approach.

This sort of integrated approach is particularly important in today's crowded classrooms, where it must be tailored as much as possible to meet the needs of each child. However, experienced teachers know that providing a truly individualized reading program for each child is simply impossible. Nevertheless, there are several options if a child is having difficulty in a particular area. One is to give the child some specific additional work to do independently. Another is to pair the child with another child who is stronger in the particular area, and have them do specific activities together. You can also inform the child's parents about the area of difficulty and send additional work home to be done with a parent's help.

Rather than focusing only on weaknesses, you also want to provide work that will encourage and help to develop particular strengths. For example, a second grader who has a strong visual memory may want to learn some poetry and will probably enjoy reciting the humorous rhymes of Ogden Nash. This sort of work can help to develop an interest in words and language, and it provides opportunities for praise and resulting increases in confidence.

Now, let's look at the specific aspects of an integrated phonics and reading program that can lead to this sort of success.

Phonics Sequence For The Year

I find that students learn best when phonic elements are taught in a particular sequence. Obviously, the amount of time needed to learn specific skills and information varies, depending on the children. Ideally, each child should have demonstrated that his or her mastery of a phonic element is automatic before proceeding to the next element. In reality, however, sometimes you will need to move ahead after several days, even if automaticity has not been achieved by each child. To keep track of each student's progress, I continue to use the Word Box and five-checkmark system described in Chapter 3 (See page 53).

Of course, your students start the year with differing backgrounds and skills, so some second graders may need to start the year reviewing material covered in first grade. For example, one year I worked with a charming second grader named Sarah, who did not have the slightest idea what a short *a* was, because her previous teacher had not taught phonics. In this sort of situation, a bright child may initially need to spend time reviewing first grade material with the least advanced reading group, but after catching up quickly may be ready for a more advanced group.

Although the starting point and amount of time on task may vary for different children, here is the teaching order of phonics I recommend for second grade:

1. Review of short vowels
2. Review of consonant digraphs *ch, th, sh, wh* (i.e., *chop, ship, this, whip*)
3. Review of initial and final consonant blends, starting with two letters and expanding to three letters (i.e., *step, pump, strip*)
4. Review of "magic *e*" rule, in which the *e* added at the end of a word makes the preceding vowel long (i.e., *lane, bride*)
5. Review of vowel digraphs, when two vowels go together, the first one says its name and the second one is silent (i.e., *dream*)
6. Word endings (*s, es, ing, est, y,* and *ed*—pronounced like a *t* as in *hoped*, a *d* as in *named*, and an *ed* as in *landed*)
7. Compound words
8. Hard and soft *c* and *g* (as pronounced in *cake, cent, gum, giraffe*)
9. Vowels before r (*er, ir, ur, ar, or*—notice that *e, i,* and *u* all have the same sound when followed by *r*)
10. Vowel digraphs and diphthongs (*oo, oi, oy, ou, ow, au, aw*—here two vowels go together, but make an entirely different sound than either one of them)
11. Syllable awareness

Achieving mastery of a particular phonic element can be a long process requiring a lot of repetition, especially for children in your lowest-level reading group. You therefore need to present the material in a number of different ways, to prevent your students from "turning off." I find that frequently changing the type of daily dictation and the educational games that reinforce the lesson can help keep your students interested.

The daily dictation is a particularly important element of every reading group lesson. When a sound is first introduced, you should dictate eight words that incorporate the sound, and then two sentences containing words that have this sound in them. The next day, you might choose to dictate five silly sentences that contain words with the sound, or a short mystery or nonsense story that contains such words. Of course, you may also find some other form of dictation that you create works well in your classroom.

But, remember that you don't want the format of the dictation to be too complicated. While you want your second graders to enjoy the learning experience, the top priority is to learn phonic skills. And, especially with weaker students, you have to present the material clearly and simply.

Additional suggestions for teaching phonics can be found in the previous chapter of this book and in Nina Traub's *Recipe for Reading*, an easy-to-use book offering methods and materials based on Orton-Gillingham principles.

The following pages contain more detailed information about specific activities and lessons that can be used to teach phonic rules and sounds to your reading groups. (There is little point in teaching a phonics lesson to the whole class, because children come to second grade with such different levels of information and skills.) As with first graders, I recommend scheduling these sorts of lessons four or even five days a week, and doing them in the morning, when children are most productive.

Sample Review Lesson For A Reading Group

This lesson is a review of material that should have been taught in first grade. Your most advanced group would probably do this right at the start of the year, or may not even need to do it at all. A mid-range group would likely be ready for it before Christmas, while your emerging readers might need to do it even later. Of course, this all depends on the ability levels and learning rates of your students.

To review the vowel digraphs, *oa* and *ai*, I first ask if anyone can name the letters that are vowels. Hopefully, more than one student does, and as a volunteer names them, I write them on the board. If no one can remember all the vowels, I say the letters myself and write them on the board.

Next, I write the word, *boat*, on the board in white chalk and tell the group that when two vowels go together, the first one says its name and the second one is silent. Another way of saying this is, "When two letters go walking, the first one does the talking." I point to the *o* and ask if anyone can say its name. When a student says it's an *o*, I emphasize that it says its name and I use colored chalk to draw a line through the *a*, which (I explain) means the *a* is silent. Then, I write *pail* on the board and ask a volunteer to come up, draw a colored line through the silent letter, and say the word. Next, I show the group some flash cards that display more *oa* and *ai* words.

As a final review before the dictation, I write four rows of words across the board. The top two rows are *oa* words and the next two rows are *ai* words. First, I ask for volunteers to read each word in a row going across the board. After all the words have been read, I ask for volunteers to read each word in a column going down the board. I praise each volunteer who does this successfully, and if a child has difficulty, I tell the child it was a good try, and then I say the word.

Depending on how well and how quickly the students are working, I might assign one or two phonics practice sheets. This helps the students review what they have learned, and it also creates an opportunity to see how they can handle independent work on this material. I use my reading notebook (I keep one for each group—see page 12) to jot down any observations or comments about particular students or the lesson itself.

Then, the children take out the phonics notebooks they use for the daily dictation. If the vowel digraphs have just been introduced, I write the digraphs on the chalkboard and remind the students to listen for them. I then might dictate eight words containing those sounds, plus a sentence or two. The next day, I try to vary the routine, perhaps by dictating a set of directions which includes words containing the digraphs, or by dictating a silly story or riddle containing them. However, with the emerging readers I try to keep the format simple, because I want them to write and see a number of words in isolation before they write a whole sentence.

If at all possible, I try to choose suitable words from books we are currently reading. Other sources include *Angling For Words* and its accompanying *Angling For Words (Sentences For Dictation)*, as well as *Recipe For Reading*.

When only the *oa* and *ai* sounds have been introduced, a sample dictation would be:

foam, float, coast, throat, chain, drain, sprain, stain

The trail led me to the railroad track.

Did the soap float and make foam?

If a reading group has poor phonics skills, I recommend that they read brief stories which help them review the sounds they are studying. *Primary Phonics Storybooks* provide suitable choices. You should also introduce all your groups to some simple trade books, which at the beginning of the year should only take a few days to read. Before we begin reading, I give the group a general introduction to what we will be reading about, as well as a preview of any words that they may find difficult. Then, the students take turns reading aloud from their copies of the book.

I try to choose a variety of books, fiction and nonfiction, because second graders are interested in so many topics. And, these days a number of publishers offer interesting paperback books for specific grade levels. I often use the book, *Hungry, Hungry Sharks*, because sharks are a popular subject and this particular book is very informative, so children enthusiastically participate in a group discussion. Another perennial favorite is the classic tale, *The Pied Piper Of Hamlin*.

If your students already know the Dolch sight words, you can use common sight words from the trade books as the group's sight words for the week. You should introduce five to seven sight words at the start of each week, depending on the ability level of your group. I write the first word on the chalkboard and ask if anyone knows it. If no one else can tell the class, I say the word. Either way, I then ask the students to write the word in the air, spelling it aloud as they write it. I then ask them to try to make a picture of it in their minds. After all the words have been introduced, I ask for a volunteer to come up and circle a specific word I name. Then, the student gets to choose a volunteer to circle another word, and so on.

Learning these words becomes a homework assignment for the students. During the reading lesson or when children are doing seat work, I or a helper check to see whether they can identify the words. At first, I hand out index cards with the words already printed on them, but as soon as the students are capable of making their own sight word cards (under supervision), I have them do the work. I put a check on each child's card each day the word is correctly identified, and when there are five checks in a row, that card goes in the "automatic" section at the back of the child's Word Box.

If possible, try to end a reading group session with a quick game. For example, you can divide the group into two teams and write a list of *oa* and *ai* words on the board. Tell the students that the answers to some riddles you are going to tell them are on the board, and then give them some riddles such as, "A _____ is hard to get. What is it?" Set a time limit, and at the end of the time the team that has answered the most riddles wins. Of course, you have to make sure to give an equal number of tries to each team.

Sample Reading Group Lesson Introducing The *oi* And *oy* Diphthongs

This lesson introducing vowel diphthongs usually would not be used until the spring. However, you may have a few advanced students who are ready for it during the fall, and you probably will have some other students who should not be introduced to diphthongs until third grade.

I introduce the lesson by saying that sometimes when two vowels are together, they make an entirely different sound than either one of their names. At first, this can be very confusing to a student who has conscientiously learned that "when two vowels go together, the first one says its name." I make sure to acknowledge this by saying something like, "This is strange, but sometimes when two vowels go together, they only make one sound, which is different than the letters you see on the page."

Providing an example is usually helpful, so I write *oil* on the board and ask if anyone can tell us the word. Usually, at least one second grader knows the answer. Then, I underline the *oi* and ask if anyone can tell us what it says, after which I write a few more *oi* words on the board and ask for volunteers to read them.

Next, I write *boy* on the board, and, of course, a lot of children can read this word. I then write a number of other *oy* words and have children read them. I point out that *oy* is usually at the end of a word (*oyster* and *royal* are exceptions), while *oi* is usually within a word. Then, we all think of others words that have these letters and sound.

About this time, I always tell my students that I was a terrible speller as a child, and I could not come up to the board and spell *oil* correctly when my teacher asked me to do it in third grade. My students are usually very impressed by this information and ask how I spelled it. I tell them that I spelled it *oile*, and I quickly add that I became a very good speller, hard as that might be to believe.

Often, my students then choose *oil* as their key word and do not forget it. They write their key words and other words on index cards which they keep in their word Word Boxes. Then, they take out their phonics notebooks, and before giving them the following dictation, I tell them that the first group of words all have either *oi* or *oy* in them:

soil, point, coin, moist, spoil, tomboy, oyster, enjoy

Can I broil the fish in tinfoil?

Roy went on a trip to Troy.

Depending on the reading group, as an enjoyable follow-up I might also dictate some silly sentences that incorporate the appropriate sounds. Examples might be

Hoist the moist coin.

Do not boil Roy in oil.

After reviewing the sentences together, ask volunteers to think of other sentences containing these sorts of words. With less advanced students, you can write words on the board for them to copy.

Phonics Activities & Games

- To support the learning process, each child should have a small spiral notebook which becomes his or her "sound book." On the front side of each page, have the children write the letter or letter combination they are studying, and on the back of the page have them draw a picture of a word that contains that sound. For example, a child studying the *oo* sound might choose to draw a picture of the moon. The word corresponding to the picture becomes the child's "key word," which the child learns to associate with a particular sound. By doing this with each new sound a child learns, the books can become wonderful resources that the children keep at their desks and refer to when not sure about a sound.

- Another supportive activity is to have the children create their own games which help them practice sounds they are studying. You can start the process by drawing a game board path and dividing it into spaces, including some surprise spaces that are fun to read. Examples might be:

"You missed your bus. Lose 1 turn."

"You won a prize. Move ahead 3 spaces."

Photocopy enough game board paths so that each child has one, and then have the children staple the pages onto manila file folders. In each space that is not already filled, the children write in words that contain sounds they are studying. These words can be copied from the board or from a list you have photocopied and distributed. Also encourage the children to decorate their game boards and obtain games pieces, small cars, or other toys to use as tokens they will move around the board.

When the game boards and tokens are ready, the children can use one die to determine how many spaces they can move along the path. Wherever they land, they must read whatever is written in the space. They can play by themselves or with other students, and they can even take the games home to play with family members.

- Second graders also enjoy playing tic-tac-toe, and it, too, can be turned into an enjoyable way to practice phonics. After photocopying and distributing a blank tic-tac-toe matrix, ask students for words that contain sounds they are studying and write those words on the board. Then, have children write a word from the board in each space. Of course, your students will put the words in different spaces and might even use some words which were not on the board.

Clear plastic can be put over the sheets, and the students can then use markers to make their *x*'s and *o*'s, after first saying the word in the space they want. When the game is done, a sponge or damp tissue can be used to clean the plastic, and the sheets can be re-used during another reading group period or during activity time, too.

- Another simple but effective game second graders enjoy is Thumbs Up, Thumbs Down. In this fast-paced sound discrimination game, the children listen to a list of words you read, putting their thumbs up if the word has a particular sound in it, or turning their thumbs down if it does not. My students always want me to keep a record of whether they are right, so I draw a column on the chalkboard for each type of word, and then put checkmarks in it as appropriate. At the end, a student tallies up the score.

- You can also use the series of games described on page 51 of the chapter on first grade and in the Resource Section. However, I find that while Let's Go Fishing is popular at the start of second grade, it loses its appeal later in the year.

Read! Read! Read!

Strong phonics skills and a good sight vocabulary are not enough to produce committed readers. Children need to find reading exciting. This sort of motivation is especially important in second grade, when reading comprehension is introduced. No matter what you do, some children are likely to have difficulty answering reading comprehension questions and writing story summaries. So, you must keep finding ways to sustain your students' enthusiasm for reading.

One important way to do this is by reading to your class every day. Hearing an absorbing story encourages your students to pick up and enjoy books by themselves. And, because second graders' horizons are expanding, they also enjoy hearing about other places and other times, as long as the information is written in an appropriate way. Now that many children are not being taught basic information at home, you also fill in important gaps when you read a variety of biographies and content-related books.

Knowing that your students' attention spans vary, start by reading books that can be completed in one or two sessions. Then, go on to short chapter books, which I always introduce to my students before I start reading. How much information I provide depends on the complexity of the story, as well as the type of students I am working with. (Introducing the characters and setting beforehand is very helpful to children who have reading comprehension or auditory problems.) And, along with chapter books, be sure to read poetry, because second graders usually love hearing the rich language and rhyming verses. Then, when you think your students are ready, begin reading longer books.

The discussions and activities that occur before and after you read are also very important. For many children, school provides the only opportunity to discuss books and other topics of interest, so your students may need additional patterning and examples. One valuable way to do this is to discuss and evaluate a chapter you have just read to the class. You and your students can talk about events and character traits, as well as make predictions about what will happen next. Like the story itself, your verbal input can serve as an excellent language model. And, your students' participation in these discussions helps them learn to express themselves—an important language skill.

Discussions like this can also help second graders learn the new "grown-up" words they often like. Words from the books you read can be written on the chalkboard and discussed. Then, you can use the words in different sentences and encourage your students to use the words in sentences they make up.

Bringing in appropriate newspaper or magazine articles to read aloud can also prompt stimulating discussions. Recently, I read an article about a new, state-of-the-art sports center to a group of second graders, who thought it was "hot" news. Two students had already been there, and they told their classmates about their experiences there. They mentioned that the facility was not fully open, so we also discussed what else might be included in it.

To encourage students to read on their own, create a stimulating library center in your classroom that provides a wide variety of books which can be read independently or with classmates. Be sure to include biographies and books about history and geography. And, because second graders are developing a new fascination with words, include poetry books, joke books, and books based on word misperceptions. Of course, mysteries and stories about the escapades of children are also popular.

Schedule a set time when children can visit the library center, which should contain magazines, as well as books. You may even want to mount some interesting articles from magazines or newspapers and put them on display, because reading an interesting piece of information in a relatively short time is very satisfying for children and encourages them do more reading.

Oral Reading

Oral reading provides second graders with intensive practice in decoding and word recognition, which helps students become fluent readers. That's why oral reading is emphasized throughout second grade and especially in the first few months of the school year, when many students are reviewing these skills.

You support students' oral reading by making sure you read aloud with each reading group every day. Your reading serves as a model for correct pronunciation, and your participation helps to quicken the reading pace, which at times can be painfully slow. You should also change your voice to make it appropriate for different characters, as this makes the reading material more interesting for students.

Oral reading can and should occur throughout the school day. In addition to being an important part of each reading group lesson you teach, it can be a natural part of other small-group and whole-class activities, or done individually or in pairs. Examples include group members reading aloud to each other during their independent reading group time, class members reading different parts of a story or play to other members of the class, and students reading virtually anything aloud to themselves or another student.

Children want to do a good job when they read aloud, so oral reading can be a terrific motivator and should be as pleasant as possible for everyone. Students who are having difficulty reading should be given only half the number of sentences to read aloud, and those sentences should be ones you are sure they can read. For these students and others, oral reading may be nerve wracking, so you should be prepared if they say their mouths are too dry and they can't speak. When this happens, I let the students have a glass water. This may be a crutch but at least it is an effective one, and as their reading progresses the students eventually don't need the water any more.

To further relieve students' stress and teach them productively, it's a good idea to preview any new material before asking students to read it. This allows you and your students to review beforehand any words that may be too difficult. Also, remember that proper nouns are often stumbling blocks, and that in some situations dyslexic students should not be required to read aloud unless you have previewed the material with them or they have volunteered to read it.

In order to keep students' oral reading smooth and enjoyable, I prefer not to interrupt or correct them, although I will softly supply a correct word when an error is made or if a child hesitates a few seconds before saying a word. I disregard unimportant errors, such as leaving off a word ending or repeating a word.

If possible, review any errors after the child finishes reading. This can be done either by focusing on whole words or on phonic elements that were previously taught. For example, second graders often substitute words that have a similar meaning, so if a student says *boat* instead of *ship*, write *ship* on the board. If the student hesitates for more than a few seconds, say the word and be sure to praise him or her for understanding the sentence. Then, explain that if the student looks carefully, he or she will see that it is a different word.

Another common error in second grade is substituting a word that looks similar. An example of this would be when a student reads *hunted* for *hinted*. In this sort of situation, help the child to read *hint* and then *hinted*. And, be sure to compliment the child when he or she uses an effective decoding strategy, as this reinforces to the child how important and useful these strategies are.

One way to increase the amount of oral reading in a class is to set up a "reading partnership" program with an older grade. In this way, second graders get to listen to more practiced readers, as well as read to them. However, be sure that your students select material they can read aloud with ease, and have them practice the selections before reading to their buddies, so they will feel more sure of themselves.

Knowing the wide range of reading levels in a second grade classroom, a natural thought might be to set up a similar program within your classroom by pairing a stronger student with a weaker students. But, I would recommend thinking very carefully about this, knowing that second graders are very self-conscious about their "image" and what their classmates think about them. Any participants need to be chosen carefully, because the additional practice may not be worth the "loss of face."

Reading Comprehension

As with oral reading, work on reading comprehension is always an important part of the morning reading group sessions and then continues to occur throughout the school day. Second graders practice this skill whenever they read books and especially when they do reading comprehension exercises included in their Learning Packets. Of course, when you read to your students during story time and then discuss the story, you are providing vital support for the development of reading comprehension skills.

Reading comprehension is not a natural skill for most second graders. At the start of the school year, it is developed primarily through the stories you and other students read aloud during reading group time. Later in the year, when students' word recognition and word analysis skills are more firmly established, you can place greater emphasis on silent reading comprehension and can have students read a selection to themselves before discussing it during their instructional group time.

I find that discussion and patterning are the most effective ways to teach reading comprehension, as you guide students to the correct interpretation of material. For example, if you want to teach students in a reading group how to find the main idea of a story, you start by asking the group, "What is this story about?" Usually, students volunteer very general answers. Then, by discussing the answers and probing further, together you consider different possibilities and narrow the topic down to a more specific answer. This teaches your students an important reading comprehension technique.

As this discussion evolves, be sure to write children's responses on the chalkboard or a chart. Seeing the ideas in writing helps students understand what is being discussed, supports their visual modality, and provides further reading practice. In addition, having a visual image clearly imprinted makes children more apt to remember how they came to their answer. Once students are comfortable with this approach, you can have them do it independently and then discuss their answers with the group.

For children who have reading comprehension difficulties, I find that discussing the characters and plot beforehand is very helpful. When appropriate, you can also stop and summarize part of a story you are reading, and have your students predict what will happen next. After you finish the story, you and your students discuss and evaluate the story, as well as the predictions. This process should include your modeling your own "thinking aloud" and encouraging your students to share their thoughts in a similar way, as this provides important support for the development of comprehension skills.

Spelling

Spelling becomes an increasingly important part of the reading/writing process as the school year advances. With your students writing full sentences and even paragraphs about what they have read, you want their written work to have fewer errors and reflect what they are learning about encoding and decoding.

Knowing that many teachers work with an established spelling program, let me just emphasize the following critical components. An effective second grade spelling program:

1. supports the development of a range of spelling skills
2. expands children's knowledge of sight words
3. teaches correct sound/symbol correspondence
4. teaches a few basic but important spelling rules that become automatic.

How should you implement this sort of program? Most spelling programs provide you with a list of sight words, but then you have to make your own decisions about how to teach them. And, because spelling is usually taught as a whole class lesson, you need to accommodate a wide range of spelling skills—something many spelling programs don't take into account.

That means you have to evaluate the sight words in terms of your individual students and probably assign five or six sight words each week. A few second graders will have difficulty mastering so many words, in which case you should only assign two or three words per week. To encourage your stronger students, you can give then one or two "bonus" words.

I strongly recommend using a kinesthetic method to teach sight words, because some students have weak visual memories that make learning the correct spelling especially difficult. You can introduce the following method to your entire class, and tell those students who don't need it that they don't have to use it. Give each child a photocopy of the spelling words for the week, with each word printed in large letters (about one-and-a-half inches tall). Tell your students to use their index fingers to trace the first word on the sheet, saying each letter as they trace it, and then say the whole word. Next, they close their eyes and see the word in their minds. The children should do this several times and then write the word without looking at the model. Next, they compare the word they have written with the sample, and if they have made an error, they repeat the process.

Correct sound/symbol correspondence is important because when this skill is secure, students start to use it for encoding and decoding. Some teachers wonder whether focusing on this will be a "waste of time" for good spellers, but I have found that some of the best readers are poor spellers who need this additional drill. The teaching order of phonics on page 97 can serve as a guide for spelling dictations—similar to your reading dictations—that you do as a whole-class activity.

In addition, I feel strongly that three key spelling rules listed below should be introduced during the second part of the year. The last two are particularly crucial and should be reviewed frequently after they are introduced.

1. The *ff, ll, ss* Rule - One-syllable words that end with *f, l,* or *s* after one vowel usually have the last letter doubled at the end (i.e., *muff, fill, mess*).

2. The Silent *e* Rule - Words ending with a silent *e* drop the *e* before a suffix beginning with a vowel, but do not drop the *e* before a suffix beginning with a consonant (i.e.,

hope, hoping, hopeful). For this and the following rule, be sure to explain what a suffix is.

3. The 1-1-1 Rule - For one-syllable words ending with one consonant after one vowel, double the final consonant before a suffix beginning with a vowel (i.e., *dim, dimmer, dimly*).

Remember that as much as possible, spelling should be an integral part of your reading program, rather than something taught in isolation. One valuable way to do this is to make your spelling sight words and examples of spelling rules part of your reading groups' dictations. And, if you come across a sight word or example of a rule in a book you are reading with a reading group, make sure to mention it or ask if anyone can find the word or example. Another variation is to write a paragraph on the board which includes appropriate sight words or examples, and then ask for volunteers to come up to the board and circle them.

Writing In Second Grade

Teaching students to express themselves on paper in an organized manner is one the most crucial and rewarding aspects of your job. Of course, you share this responsibility with your students' future teachers, but you at least need to make sure that important building blocks—which also help students further develop their reading ability—are in place.

The writing routine changes markedly after first grade, because most students can now handle a more challenging curriculum. While second graders continue to write in their Story Notebooks, other important activities now become part of the routine. Perhaps most important is that students' growing maturity enables them to become more active participants in the writing process through conferencing, editing, and proofreading.

The Writing Process

There are now so many wonderful books about the writing process, I want to focus here on just a few key elements:

Discussing the topic - Doing this before a student actually begins writing can be extremely helpful, as verbalizing is easier than writing for many children. Of course, with a large class you don't always have time to do this on an individual basis, so you might need to lead a class or group discussion. Another alternative is assigning "story partners," who discuss the topic with each other.

Conferencing - This is usually introduced in second grade. Before writing, students talk with the teacher or each other about what they want to write and how to go about it. After writing, the students can discuss whether they succeeded and are satisfied with their work. Early in the year, you probably need to role play a conference with a student in front of the class, so your students learn how to conduct themselves. Then, you may have each child's story partner also serve as a conference partner, or a few students can have a conference together. But, you should also try to meet with each student for a few minutes each week.

Editing - When the time comes for your students to act as editors, let them know that they should first see if the ideas are clear. And, because many second graders are not yet experts on the mechanics of writing, remind them that when they are reviewing a story, they should check for necessary capital letters, correct punctuation and spelling, and legible handwriting. (Keep a list of these points prominently displayed in the classroom.) As this is a learning experience for the editor, as well as the writer, you may decide to focus only on certain aspects at first.

In the long run, it's usually more beneficial for children to discover their own errors. If a student is having a hard time finding an error, you can provide a hint. And, when students have difficulty with sentence structure or their thoughts are unclear, you might ask them to read their work aloud. This often helps them identify the problem, and then we discuss it together. I only correct what I think second graders should know, and I make sure they realize how valuable and unique their writing is.

Proofreading - Proofreading skills should be introduced one-by-one through a series of class lessons. I find that just as second graders enjoy learning the rules of a new game, they can also enjoy learning the rules of writing. In regard to spelling errors, I provide examples of a letter reversal (*b/d*) and a letter order error (*clean/claen*). I ask the children to think about the type of errors they make and which types they make the most, so they know to watch for them when proofreading.

Paragraph Writing

During the second half of second grade, you can introduce an important new topic—paragraph writing. The goal for this year is to teach children how to write a basic paragraph comprised of a topic sentence, three supporting sentences, and a concluding sentence. I find that the key to teaching this skill is a step-by-step approach, in which you have to go slowly and make sure your students understand each step before proceeding to the next.

When I introduce paragraph writing, I tell my students how proud I am that they are ready to learn how to write a paragraph. Then, I hand out composition books and tell the children that these are their "paragraph notebooks," which they will soon feel as proud of as their Story Notebooks. I explain that a paragraph is a group of sentences that are all about one subject, and I show some examples on the chalkboard, which I read aloud or we read aloud together. We then discuss how all the sentences relate to the paragraph's subject. (A good source of simple paragraphs is *Specific Skills Series: Getting the Main Idea* (B).)

The next step is learning how to formulate related ideas. At first, the entire class makes simple lists together, using categories such as favorite books or things that are soft. Then, I divide the class into groups, each of which has an assigned scribe, and I ask the groups to make simple lists. They have five minutes to make their lists, and when the time is up, a group member reads the list to the class. I write some of the lists on the board, and we brainstorm appropriate headings, as shown below:

basketball	marshmallows	hamburgers
hockey	snow	corn
football	milk	carrots
tennis	clouds	beans
(sports)	(white things)	(foods)

Using their paragraph notebooks, your students can practice creating lists and deciding on topic headings during their independent reading group time. When they demonstrate that they can do this sort of exercise, you can introduce the concept of a topic and supporting sentences, by writing a paragraph such as the following on the board:

My sister is great! She helps me with my homework. She tells funny jokes. She lets me play with her friends.

Read this paragraph to the class, and identify the topic sentence by underlining it with colored chalk. Explain that the topic sentence tells what the main idea of the paragraph is, while the supporting sentences support or explain the topic sentence. Then, write a few other paragraphs on the board and ask for student volunteers to read the paragraphs and underline the topic sentences.

When your students can do this, write a topic sentence on the chalkboard and then ask the class to think of reasons that support the sentence. (A sample topic might be: *Dogs are wonderful pets.*) While the students brainstorm, write their reasons as phrases on the chalkboard. Next, you and your students decide what order you want the reasons in, and you then number them accordingly. This becomes the outline for the paragraph. After that, you can read the outline phrases and explain how to turn them into complete sentences, which you identify as supporting sentences and write under the topic sentence.

Once your students know how to do this, have them copy a topic sentence from the board into their notebooks. (For example, *Summer vacations are lots of fun.*) Have the class brainstorm ideas, which you write on the board. After the ideas are numbered and volunteers turn the outline phrases into complete sentences, the children copy these sentences into their notebooks.

The next step is to start giving your students topic sentences, and have the students supply their own supporting sentences. This becomes a regular assignment, which your students can practice individually, in teams, or in groups.

Then, you teach your students how to write a topic sentence, which you can do by writing three supporting sentences on the board and having your class brainstorm possible topic sentences. Here's an example:

*Topic sentence:*_____.
There are seals in outdoor pools.
Monkeys are swinging from trapezes.
Lions and tigers are in cages.

This can be a challenging activity, so I find it works best when done as a group lesson. And, remember that paragraph writing is a slow progression, which is not completed in one week. Depending on the class, your students might start on this in January or February and continue through the end of the year.

Finally, it is time to introduce the concluding sentence. I explain that this sentence is an ending sentence that explains what the paragraph has talked about. I read a complete, sample paragraph (see below) I have written on the board, and we discuss why the concluding sentence is appropriate. Then, I ask the students to think up other possible concluding sentences.

Topic sentence: I have a great room.
Supporting sentences: 1. My bed is very soft.
                         2. I have lots of room for my things.
                         3. I have a soft rug to sit on.
Concluding sentence: My room is the best place in the house.

Next, show your students paragraphs that lack concluding sentences, and have the students dictate to you several possible concluding sentences. Then, divide your class in groups, each of which has an assigned scribe and students of varying ability. Give each group a paragraph which lacks a concluding sentence, and tell the groups to brainstorm and write a concluding sentence, which will then be read to the other groups.

Writing paragraphs together can then become a whole class activity, which is done repeatedly. You can provide a number of topics and let your students choose the one they want to write about, or just provide assigned topics.

Toward the end of the year, your students will start writing paragraphs more independently. You can divide the class into pairs and give them all the same assignment. On one page of their paragraph notebooks, the students jot down their ideas and number them. On the opposite page, they turn these ideas into supporting sentences. Then, they write their topic and concluding sentences. The partners help each other, while you circulate and supervise.

On the following day, have the children edit their work with their partners or in groups. You may also decide to devote more sessions to this assignment, depending on your class. And, during a final session or during the child's conference time with you, you can review the paragraph together.

At the end of the year, I have an individual conference with each child. We review the paragraph notebook, and I make sure to praise the child and point out how much he or she has learned. We have a "paragraph tea" to which parents are invited, and the students read their favorite paragraphs.

Integrating Reading & Writing

Throughout the year, writing activities are an integral part of students' reading group time. And, as the year progresses, this integration increases through students reading what they have written and writing about what they have read. The story and paragraph notebooks are important parts of this process, which extends into other times of the day and other subject areas.

Utilizing second graders' curiosity about the world around them can be particularly effective in this regard. For example, setting up a pen pal program with a school in a different country can become a combined reading/writing project that captures students' interest and stimulates them to use newly learned skills. One second grade teacher I know arranged for her class to be pen pals with a second grade class in England. Her students were eager to read their pen pals' letters and took pride in writing their own. The teacher supported their interest by reading some short, informative books about England during story time, as well as stories written by English authors. After dividing the students into pairs and making sure that struggling readers had competent readers as partners, this enterprising teacher also had the students read appropriate books about England or by English writers. And, a highlight of the entire project was a formal English tea arranged by the teacher and parent volunteers!

Language Development

To support their continued progress as readers, most second graders also need to strengthen their language skills by further developing their vocabulary and general facility with words. You can accomplish this by continuing and building on the language development program that was started in first grade (and described on pages 59-64). Categorization, similarities and differences, part/whole relationships, and antonyms all remain important and need further work, as you introduce more challenging words and concepts.

At first, this work is primarily presented orally and discussed as a class or in groups. When appropriate, you should also use your chalkboard, so that your students can hear and see the material. And, once students understand a concept, they should also complete practice sheets that reinforce the skill. Depending on the assignment, these sheets may be completed by students working with partners or in groups, as well as individually.

Many of the oral activities are enjoyable and can be scheduled for either the morning or afternoon. Some don't take very long and can be done while waiting to go to the lunchroom or playground. In addition, many of the games described in the chapter on first grade remain popular and effective educational activities in second grade.

Here's a brief summary of some key points and activities to consider:

Categorization

Ask your students to list related items, and gradually increase the number of items, while making the categories more specific. For example, together you can make lists of foods that start with a certain letter. Or, make separate lists of summer and winter sports.

Then, you can move on to more challenging types of categorizations. Write *steak, green beans, carrots,* and *spinach* on the board, and then ask which three belong together and why. Next, write or say two words, such as *saw* and *hammer,* and ask the class how they are related, as well as how many others like them the class members can think of. You can also make lists of contrasting categories, as when you write the headings *things in the sky* and *things underground* on the board, and then have the class see which category will win by having the most items under its heading.

Similarities & Differences

Making these sorts of distinctions can be a challenging task for children, so I recommend starting with simple items. And, especially in the beginning, having the students see actual objects can be very helpful. Possibilities include:

coloring book and comic book,
adhesive tape and glue,
tennis racket and bat,
soap and toothpaste.

You may decide to list how the items are similar and different, but it is not necessary to do this all the time.

Part/Whole Relationships

Exploring these relationships is important conceptually and also a wonderful way for children to learn new vocabulary words. One effective approach is to show your students a picture of something like a car or a plane, and ask them to name the parts. For a change of pace, make a list of the parts and ask for a volunteer who can identify the whole object (i.e., a table, menu, or stove).

Antonyms

Gradually, ask your second graders to identify the opposites of increasingly difficult words. The games described in the antonym section of the previous chapter are just as popular and effective in second grade. And, like first graders, second graders enjoy creating stories using antonym pairs.

Excellent sources for the word lists needed to work with antonyms in this way include *Language Remediation and Expansion, 150 Skill Building Reference Lists,* and *HELP - Handbook of Exercises for Language Processing, Volume 2.*

Homonyms

Second graders love knowing something that they think is "grown-up," so you may want to present the following activities as a way of learning this sort of information. Explain to the class that some words sound alike but are spelled differently and have different meanings, and these words are called homonyms. Then, write the word *rode* and ask for a volunteer who can use it in a sentence. A child will probably say something like, "I rode a horse." Next, ask if any-one knows another word that sounds alike but is spelled differently and has a different mean-ing. After someone answers, write *road* on the board and ask who can use it in a sentence.

If some of your students have difficulty with this process, make sure to write the sen-tences on the board. Also, use a prominent place to display a chart listing homonyms the class has discovered, and periodically add more words to it.

Similes

With their new-found appreciation of language, second graders are ready to learn about similes. You may want to start by writing a few well-known similes on the board, such as *white as a sheet* or *big as a house.* You can then can explain that similes compare and explain things using the words *like* or *as.* You may also want to read some examples taken from literature, such as "I wandered lonely as a cloud..." from William Wordsworth's poem of the same name, or "He felt like the peanut butter part of a sandwich, squeezed between Mike and Ellen," from Judy Blume's *The One in the Middle is the Green Kangaroo.*

As with homonyms, you can keep a simile chart which you add to when students come across similes in their reading. And, I find that children enjoy making up their own similes. To encourage them, you can create a "simile tree" on a bulletin board and have a box of blank "leaves" underneath, which students can use to write their similes on and then attach to the tree. Second graders enjoy watching the tree grow, and it provides a good opportunity for you to make comments about their growing use of language.

You and your students can also compose simile sentences together. For example, have your students discuss and fill in:

"My pet was_____."
"_____as slow as molasses."
"_____as light as a feather."

Vocabulary Building

Second graders enjoy creating stories together, and this can be a wonderful way for your students to use new vocabulary words that they would not otherwise use on their own. As a story starter, write some "describing" words from stories you have read with the class. Also write the first few sentences of a story, and then ask your students to think up additional sentences containing the describing words on the board.

Another way to enlarge second graders' vocabulary is to bring in an interesting object and have the class brainstorm words to describe it. Then, you may want to have the class write a story together using those words.

As their oral language skills improve, there is often a noticeable change in second graders' speaking vocabulary and verbal fluency. With encouragement, this can strengthen their self-esteem, and the new-found fluency can transfer to their writing skills, as well. Following are some combined language and writing activities that I recommend to support this process. Of course, you should discuss these activities with the class before assigning them as independent or group work.

1. Write a story extension on the chalkboard with your class. Then, have each of your students write their own extension of another story, after which they can read their extensions to the rest of the class. This part of the activity should be divided into two sessions, as children lose interest when they have too many stories to listen to. The entire activity can also be done as a group activity, with one student assigned to be responsible for handling any questions that arise.

2. Write a sentence on the board and show your class how the sentence can be improved by adding, deleting, or substituting words. For example, if you write, "The class went on a trip to the zoo," you and your students can brainstorm adjectives that would make the sentence more lively and informative. After doing a few of these exercises together, you can assign sentences for students to do on their own, with a partner, or with a group.

3. Show your second graders how they can expand a sentence by using conjunctions. Write the conjunctions *so, and, but* on the board, along with a sentence such as "I was sick." Ask for volunteers to expand the sentence using the conjunctions. Then, tell your students that they will each expand sentences on their own and read them aloud. Hand out practice sheets containing starter sentences and a choice of conjunctions for sentence expansion.

4. Have your students make up their own sentences, based on some sentence starters you write on the board (*Tomorrow...*, *Sometimes...*, *Last night...*). Second graders are often amazed at how many different sentences they can create. After they have done this a few times, show the children how they can improve their sentences by adding, deleting, or substituting words. This a wonderful exercise for students to do as groups or teams, and it should include the students reading their work to their classmates.

5. Have your students write statements, commands, and questions, and encourage them to use their imagination. For example, write a sentence on the board such as, "I ate ten pieces of pizza in eight minutes." Then, ask the class what silly statements they can think of. This makes a practice session fun, and once second graders grow used to writing and then reading sentences in this way, they can do it as a class, in a small group, or with a partner.

Developing Auditory Skills

To strengthen second graders' auditory skills, you need a program which develops their auditory discrimination, as well as their auditory memory. I've found that the following program can be very effective and needs to be done for only fifteen or twenty minutes a few times a week.

In my experience, many second graders still don't how to listen well, so this is an important skill to teach. Most students can easily hear the beginning and ending sounds of a word, but more than a few have difficulty hearing the medial sounds. To help them, tell your students to listen for a particular sound in the middle of a word ("Does the word *summer* have the *m* sound in the middle?") and raise their hands if they hear it. *HELP 1—Handbook of Exercises for Language Processing* is a good source of words to use for this type of exercise.

During the same sessions in which your students are practicing this skill, you can also have them practice sound blending. Start with three-phoneme words (*wr-e-ck*) and then move to four- and five-phoneme words (*p-e-pp-er, j-a-ck-e-t*).

As part of the process of increasing listening awareness, your students need to learn what a syllable is, if they haven't already. I tell students they are going to learn a word that is usually for older children. Then, I write the word *syllable* on the board and explain what is. We practice finding the syllables in two- and three-syllable words until the class understands the concept. Once you have accomplished this, you can do exercises such as saying a three- or four-syllable word and asking the children what the second syllable is. Or, you can say a word and ask how many syllables are in it. (For second grade, you should only go up to four-syllable words.) You can find appropriate words for these exercises in *Language Remediation and Expansion—150 Skill Building Reference Lists*.

Along with their work on auditory discrimination, second graders often need help developing their auditory memories. There are activities you can use to practice several related skills at the same time, but it is important to go slowly and make sure the exercises do not become too challenging, so your students don't start feeling defeated.

To strengthen students' short-term memories, say, "Let's see how many words you can remember. Listen carefully to what I say, and then I will ask you to tell me the words after I have finished." Start with three or four words from the same category (*pants, shirt, sock, shoe*). You are likely to find that a few students will even be able to remember five words. Once your students can remember four related words, start giving them lists of unrelated words (*rock, pen, clock, tree*). Unrelated words are much harder to remember, so you may want to suggest that your students make a picture in their mind of each word when you read it. *HELP 1 - Handbook of Exercises for Language Processing* has lists of these sorts of words.

Another popular and important exercise is remembering a set of oral directions in sequential order. You can structure this sort of exercise so that your students can do them individually when seated, or you can pick a volunteer or two who will follow the directions around the room. First, explain you are going to tell them some things to do, and that they must listen carefully and do just what they are told. Start with two-stage directions and quickly move up to three-stage directions. Four-stage directions are the limit for second graders. To an entire class, you might say, "Put your hand on your head. Stick out your tongue. Wiggle your nose." For a volunteer, you can try, "Open the door. Jump two times. Make a *b* on the chalkboard."

You also want to improve your students' recall of stories and information. Your daily reading is very important in this regard, and I would recommend that you read short paragraphs to your class, then ask them to summarize orally what you have read. You can find interesting and appropriate paragraphs in a weekly reader, a children's magazine, or a trade book.

Having developed and strengthened a wide variety of language skills during second grade, your students should be ready to continue progressing successfully in third grade.

CHAPTER 5

Becoming A Third Grade Reading Specialist

In third grade, the curriculum begins to shift from "learning to read" to "reading to learn." Third graders must not only continue to consolidate and perfect the decoding and other skills introduced in earlier grades, they must also start learning basic comprehension skills that will help them use reading as a means of gathering information.

This important part of the third grade curriculum provides vital preparation for the demands of fourth grade and beyond. It's also one of the reasons that the gap between competent and at-risk readers becomes more noticeable during this school year. One principal said to me, "This is the year that all the plugs should be pulled out to help these kids. After third grade, it's too late." While I believe this statement is a little strong, I agree with the underlying message. Helping third graders overcome reading problems is crucial to the students' future success, and if the problems extend into fourth grade, they become markedly harder to remediate.

In addition to some third graders who still have difficulty "cracking the code," you are likely to find that other students start to have difficulty with comprehension, as their reading assignments become increasingly abstract and the language becomes more complex. To help these and all your students, immerse them in rich language experiences. Read books that have lush and varied language, and make sure to focus on the setting, characters, and your students' predictions before discussing the stories. Knowing that the way you speak serves as an important model for your students, make sure to use interesting language yourself. All this is particularly important for students growing up with the paucity of televised language.

As in first and second grades, the "game plan" for third grade must be tailored to meet the needs and pace of individual learners. Some children—usually including weaker readers—

forget certain skills during the long summer break, so a review of some of the work covered in second grade will be essential. Your informal evaluation of your students at the start of the school year will help you determine which students need review work and what they need to review. In general, you should make sure to review the short vowel sounds, as students often mix these up to the detriment of their reading, as well as their spelling.

In addition, students need to enlarge their sight vocabulary. And, they must also develop their "chunking" skills in both reading and spelling, so that they can automatically recognize common prefixes (*re, in, inter*) and suffixes (*ing, ed, ful*). Basic syllabification rules should also be introduced as soon as possible and then practiced on a regular basis throughout the year.

Reading aloud continues to be part of each reading lesson. Be sure to note when children omit necessary word endings, and use your own examples to show how these omissions can change the meaning of a sentence (*I sip my soda* or *I sipped my soda.* Is it happening now or has it already been done?) This can also provide opportunities to check on your students' sense of time, which can affect their understanding of words such as *before, after, often, sometimes, yesterday, today,* and *tomorrow.* A lack of understanding of these basic concepts can undermine their reading comprehension and their writing. The same holds true for your students' understanding of hours, minutes, and seconds. You may be surprised, as I often am, at the number of third graders who still have trouble telling time without a digital watch.

As your students' oral reading skills improve, ask them to do more silent reading. Your goal is to teach them to obtain information from a text by themselves, and in order for them to do this, you must help them develop a full range of language, writing, and spelling skills. This can be accomplished through systematic instruction and practice, combined with enrichment and—when necessary—remediation.

Writing is a particularly important part of this process, and third grade is the year to develop students' paragraph writing skills, which were introduced in second grade (see pages 109-112). This year, you want all your students to learn to write simple, clear paragraphs, while some of your more proficient third graders proceed to elaborate on their supporting ideas and write fuller paragraphs.

My overall strategy for achieving these goals remains the same as in first and second grade:

1. Evaluate your students' skills and abilities, and use this information as the basis for forming your reading groups.

2. Implement an organized, sequential learning program.

3. Teach your students to work independently as well as in groups.

4. Use an integrated approach that combines phonics and whole language techniques.

Evaluating Third Graders' Reading

To obtain baseline information about your students' reading skills and abilities at the start of the school year, you'll want to talk to your students individually and administer a series of brief evaluations, including a short silent reading test. This will provide you with a basic understanding of your students' knowledge of general information, their "word attack" skills, their oral and silent reading, and their auditory comprehension.

Additional information about this sort of evaluation can be found in the previous chapter (see pages 67-84). However, the third grade evaluation is longer and includes two new sections—a paragraph with accompanying comprehension questions that you read to each student, and a silent reading test that you administer to the whole class. This evaluation is also different because it does not ask students to identify consonant sounds or name lower case letters, as most third graders can now accomplish these tasks.

I find that a good way to begin the evaluation is asking the general information questions, which children usually do not find threatening. Questions about what day and month it is—and which ones come next—reveal whether children usually know and remember this information—and have a sufficiently developed sense of time to know what will follow. In a similar way, asking what month comes before August reveals whether a student knows the months of the year in order and can retrieve the information.

The question, "What should you do if you want to find the meaning of a word?", can reveal a variety of different types of information. Does the student remember the word, *dictionary*? If not, does he or she describe the book or propose an alternative method—and does that make sense? The student's handling of this question provides information about his or her vocabulary, general knowledge, and thinking process.

To evaluate the child's language skills, you ask the child to tell you how soap and toothpaste are the same, and how they are different. In regard to similarities, the child might say that both are found in the bathroom. Or, a higher-level response would be that they both help keep you clean. You also ask what a telescope is, and you can expect a similar variety of answers, ranging from "something you look through" to "something that makes things that are far away seem close." The more precise the child's answers, the less probing and modeling of the thinking process you will need to do during the year.

Next, you read aloud a paragraph at a third grade reading level and ask the student a few comprehension questions. Essentially, you want to find out whether the child can answer the questions, and if not, why is the child having difficulty? Does it appear to be an auditory processing problem or a language problem?

Third Grade Reading Evaluation
For durability I suggest that you mount the different parts of the test on large index cards.

Nonsense Words

Tests 3-6

rab	ped	vin	mog	lub
bave	mede	lipe	sobe	tule
preal	sloam	stail	smeef	tway	skoe
chark	smer	floy	plor	slaw	thow

Sight Words

funny	every
four	there
pretty	after
want	once
could	draw

The Oral Reading Test

Mom and I live in a big city.
One day we go for a walk.
We see many cars on the street.
"I like the red car," says Mom.
"I like the pretty blue car," I say.
We see boys and girls playing.
They play ball in a small lot.

I help my mother and father.
I work in the house.
When my little sister cries I play with her.
Then she laughs.
I walk our big black dog Spot.
I go to the store for milk.
One day I helped my Dad.
I cut the grass and helped Dad cut down a tree.

When my sister had her birthday Mom and Dad bought her a puppy. What a puppy it was! Sometimes my sister would let me play with the puppy. I dreamed about it! How I wanted one of my own.

Then on my birthday they bought me one, too. They even gave me a dish and a toy for the puppy. It was the happiest day.

Williamsburg is a very famous city in Virginia. People from all over go there to see it.

Much of Williamsburg has been made to look just as it did in the 1700s, when it was the capital of the state. Some buildings that had burned down have been rebuilt. Men and women dressed in clothes like those worn in the 1700s welcome the visitors. They tell how people lived and worked in those early times.

Reprinted by permission of Educators Publishing Service.

Karl Wallenda was the most famous high-wire walker in circus history. Sadly, he was killed in 1978. While he was walking on a 75 foot cable strung between two buildings, a gust of wind made him lose his balance.

Karl was born into a circus family in Germany in 1905. His father was a catcher in a flying trapeze act. As children Karl and his brother performed acrobatic stunts in front of restaurants, and people threw money in a hat for them.

While he was still a boy, he joined a high-wire act. At seventeen he was so good that he had his own act.

Reprinted by permission of Educators Publishing Service.

Informal Test - Student Record Sheet

Student's Name: _____

Date: _____

Age: _____

I. General Information

1. What day is today? _____

2. What day is tomorrow? _____

3. What month is after this month? _____

4. What month comes before August? _____

5. What should you do if you want to find
   the meaning of a word? _____

6. How are soap and toothpaste alike
   and how are they different? _____

7. What is a telescope? _____

II. Auditory Listening Comprehension Passage

Elizabeth Blackwell was the first woman doctor of modern times. She was born in 1821 and came to the United States when she was eleven years old.

In those days girls did not usually get the same education as boys. However, her father believed that girls should also have a good education.

Elizabeth Blackwell became a schoolteacher, but she did not like teaching. She wanted to become a doctor. There had never been a female doctor in the United States since medical schools would not admit women. Finally, Geneva Medical College in New York admitted her, and she graduated at the top of her class.

Reprinted by permission of Educators Publishing Service.

1. Why is Elizabeth Blackwell famous? _____
   She was the first woman doctor.

2. How did her father help Elizabeth? _____
   He let her have a good education.

3. Before she became a doctor, what did Elizabeth Blackwell do? _____
   She was a schoolteacher.

III. Informal Reading Skills Test

1. The Rhyming Test

Sample: What word rhymes with Dad? If the student cannot think of a word, supply one.

Tell me a word that rhymes with

hat   _____

bake   _____

jail   _____

heat   _____

Number Correct: _____

2. Sound blending
   Pronounce as shown in first column. Have the student try again, if the first response is incorrect. Note both answers. Give full credit, if the second attempt is correct.

    1. s-o   (so)   _____

    2. sh-oe   (shoe)   _____

    3. ch-arm   (charm)   _____

    4. t-oo-th   (tooth)   _____

    5. m-i-l-k   (milk)   _____

6. p-e-pp-er   (pepper)   _____

Number Correct: _____

3. Short Vowel Words

   1. rab   _____

   2. ped   _____

   3. vin   _____

   4. mog   _____

   5. lub   _____

   Number Correct: _____

4. The Magic e Words

   1. bave   _____

   2. mede   _____

   3. lipe   _____

   4. sobe   _____

   5. tule   _____

   Number Correct: _____

5. Two Vowels Together Words

   1. preal   _____

   2. sloam   _____

   3. stail   _____

   4. smeef   _____

   5. tway   _____

6. skoe _____

Number Correct: _____

6. Vowels Before R And Vowel Diphthong Words

1. chark _____

2. smer _____

3. floy _____

4. plor _____

5. slaw _____

6. thow _____

Number Correct: _____

7. Sight Words

1. funny _____

2. four _____

3. pretty _____

4. want _____

5. could _____

6. every _____

7. there _____

8. after _____

9. once _____

10. draw _____

Number Correct: _____

IV. The Oral Reading Test And Checklist

Primer

Mom and I live in a big city.

One day we go for a walk.

We see many cars on the street.

"I like the red car," says Mom.

"I like the pretty blue car," I say.

We see boys and girls playing.

They play ball in a small lot.

Errors: _____

Grade 1

I help my mother and father.

I work in the house.

When my little sister cries I play with her.

Then she laughs.

I walk our big black dog Spot.

I go to the store for milk.

One day I helped my Dad.

I cut the grass and helped Dad cut down a tree.

Errors: _____

Grade 2

When my sister had her birthday Mom and Dad bought her a puppy. What a puppy it was! Sometimes my sister would let me play with the puppy. I dreamed about it! How I wanted one of my own.

Then on my birthday they bought me one, too. They even gave me a dish and a toy for the puppy. It was the happiest day.

Errors: _____

Grade 3

Williamsburg is a very famous city in Virginia. People from all over go there to see it.

Much of Williamsburg has been made to look just as it did in the 1700s, when it was the capital of the state. Some buildings that had burned down have been rebuilt. Men and women dressed in clothes like those worn in the 1700s welcome the visitors. They tell how people lived and worked in those early times.

Reprinted by permission of Educators Publishing Service.

Errors: _____

Grade 4

Karl Wallenda was the most famous high-wire walker in circus history. Sadly, he was killed in 1978. While he was walking on a 75 foot cable strung between two buildings, a gust of wind made him lose his balance.

Karl was born into a circus family in Germany in 1905. His father was a catcher in a flying trapeze act. As children Karl and his brother performed acrobatic stunts in front of restaurants, and people threw money in a hat for them.

While he was still a boy, he joined a high-wire act. At seventeen he was so good that he had his own act.

Reprinted by permission of Educators Publishing Service.

Errors: _____

Checklist of Type of Errors Made

_____ mispronunciations

_____ hesitations

_____ repetitions

_____ omissions

_____ additions

Additional comments:

Approximate Oral Reading Level: _____

V. Silent Reading Test

Passage 1: The Indians Who Breathe Thin Air

Air goes up for thousands of miles. The higher the air, the thinner it gets. Then air is hard to breathe. People who go up into high mountains often get dizzy. Breathing the thin air makes them dizzy.

Airplanes fly more than 15,000 feet above the sea. The air is very thin. Are the pilots dizzy? No. They breathe oxygen from a tank.

In South America, Indians live far up on the mountains. Their homes are more than 15,000 feet above the sea. The air is thin. The Indians are not breathing oxygen from a tank. But they do not get dizzy. They have lived in these mountains all their lives. Their lungs have changed. They have become larger. The large lungs help the Indians breathe the thin air.

Sometimes the Indians go down to the low country. People living down there feel fine. But the Indians feel sick.

1. People who go up high in the mountains often get
   a. sleepy.   c. hungry.
   b. tired.   d. dizzy.

2. The word in the story that means something that holds oxygen is _____.

3. The story says, "People who go up into high mountains often get dizzy. Breathing the thin air makes them dizzy." The word *them* means _____.

4. Which of the following does this story lead you to believe?
   a. People get used to the air where they live.
   b. Air is found only in tanks.
   c. Breathing is hard for the mountain Indians.

5. The main idea of the story is that
   a. Indians like to fly over mountains.
   b. mountain Indians can breathe thin air.
   c. airplanes can fly high over mountains.

6. The opposite of small (paragraph three, sentence nine) is _____.

Reprinted by permission of Phoenix Learning Resources.

Passage 2: Meet the Cactus

When are a bunny's ears green? When does a rat's tail grow in a basket?

Was your answer "When it is a cactus plant?" If so, you are right! Plants that belong to the cactus family are special. Cactus plants can live for weeks without being watered. They store extra water in their roots and stems.

The cactus plant is a green plant. Like other green plants, it uses sunlight to make food. It makes its food in its stem. The body of the cactus is usually covered with spines. These spines can be soft and hairy. Or they can be hard and pointed like a needle. Also, all cactus plants have some type of flower.

There are hundreds of different kinds of cactus plants. Some, like the "living rock" cactus, are small and almost round. Others, like the "bunny ears" cactus, can grow quite tall and wide. And still other cactus plants, like the "rat tail," grow long, thin stems that hang down.

1. A cactus is
   a. an animal.
   b. a plant.
   c. a flower.

2. A cactus plant is special because it
   a. is tall and wide.
   b. has spines.
   c. can store water.

3. The cactus plant is like other green plants because it
   a. has scratchy spines that are like needles.

b. has no flowers.

c. uses sunlight to make its own food.

4. The food is made in the _____ of the cactus.
   a. stem
   b. spines
   c. roots

5. Cactus plant are good plants to grow in places where
   a. there is a lot of rain.
   b. there is very little rain.
   c. it is always dry.

Reprinted by permission of Phoenix Learning Resources.

Passage 3: Tumbleweeds, Rolling Weeds

Tumbleweeds often roll into all the wrong places.

A weed is a plant that grows just about anywhere, especially in places where it is not wanted. The tumbleweed is a kind of weed, a "rolling weed."

A tumbleweed may grow to be I to 2 meters high. In the fall of the year, the dry, brittle stem of the tumbleweed breaks off at the ground, and that is when the tumbleweeds become real pests. Tumbleweeds are blown easily by the wind, and when they begin to roll, they seem to stop in all the wrong places. They roll into highway fences and pile up, one on top of the other. They roll into backyards and even pile up in swimming pools!

What can be done to hold back the growth of these rolling weeds? Scientists have found a moth that eats tumbleweed. They hope that this moth will keep down the number of tumbleweeds so that the rolling weed will not be such a pest.

1. The word weed is used to describe
   a. an unwanted plant.
   b. a plant that is hard to grow.
   c. a rolling plant.

2. What causes tumbleweeds to break off at the stem?
   a. They grow too tall.
   b. They become dry and brittle.
   c. Moths eat them.

3. What do scientists hope will cut down on the growth of tumbleweeds?
   a. moths

b. fences
c. wind

4. Which sentence below tells you that tumbleweeds are pests?
   a. A tumbleweed is a kind of plant.
   b. Tumbleweeds pile up in people's yards.
   c. Tumbleweeds are found in North America.

5. Why do you think tumbleweeds roll so easily?
   a. because they are light in weight
   b. because they are a kind of weed
   c. because they are pests

   Reprinted by permission of Phoenix Learning Resources.

Passage 4: The Flashlight Fish

Have you ever seen a fish with its very own lights?

Some fish have built-in lights. That is, the lights are actually a part of the fish's body! One such fish lives in the Red Sea. It is called the "flashlight fish" because it has special body parts, or organs, that give off light. The flashlight fish has one light organ underneath each eye. These lights are bright and greenish in color, and they are always "on." But a flashlight fish can conceal, or hide, its lights by raising an extra piece of skin up over each organ. Then, when the fish lowers the skin, the lights can be seen again.

What purpose do these special lights have? The light organs help the fish locate food at night along the Red Sea reefs. They also help the fish escape from its enemies. Usually, the lights are flashed "on" and "off" about once every 20 seconds. But when the fish is upset, it will blink its lights about 75 times in 1 minute. Can you imagine 20 or 30 flashlight fish blinking their lights all at the same time?

1. In this story, the word organ means
   a. an extra piece of skin.
   b. a special body part.
   c. a kind of eye.

2. The flashlight fish uses its lights to hunt for food and to
   a. change color.
   b. conceal its eyes.
   c. escape from enemies.

3. The flashlight fish gets its name from its
   a. greenish color.
   b. special organs.
   c. unusual eyes.

4. When a flashlight fish is upset, its lights will
   a. be covered.
   b. flash faster.
   c. turn bright green.

5. If a flashlight fish were looking for food at night, it would probably
   a. lower its special piece of skin.
   b. turn green in color.
   c. look for flashing lights.

Reprinted by permission of Phoenix Learning Resources.

Passage 1: Number Correct: _____

Passage 2: Number Correct: _____

Passage 3: Number Correct: _____

Passage 4: Number Correct: _____

Comments:

Then comes the Informal Reading Skills Evaluation, which I introduce by explaining that this will help me understand what the student learned in second grade and what we should work on this year. I also point out that I do not expect the child to know everything I ask. An anxious child needs this reassurance, and supportive remarks help keep all students involved and at ease, so I praise each child's performance (even it is weak) in order to encourage an optimal performance.

The first sub-test asks a student to think of two words that rhyme with the test word. Most third graders complete this task easily, but there are always a few who do not. They need additional help with rhyming and may have trouble working with "families" of words that sound alike.

For the sub-tests that follow, I recommend writing down and analyzing students' errors. In particular, note how the student approaches each task, as this tells you a lot about the student's word attack skills. Does the child try to decode words or rely on sight memory? The answer tells you which approach the child favors and where he or she is likely to need additional help.

If the student cannot answer at least one of the first three questions in subtests 2-6, I move right on to the next section. The student's weak performance has already shown that he or she needs additional help with this sort of work.

Subtests 2-5 tap skills that are usually covered in a first grade curriculum and reviewed during second grade. Please see pages 67-84 for an explanation of how to administer and interpret these subtests. Subtest 6 shows whether a child has a good working knowledge of diphthongs and the sounds of vowels preceding the letter, *r*. These skills are often covered in a second grade phonics curriculum. Subtest 7 reveals the child's knowledge of some basic sight words. Mastery would be 5 out of 6 for Subtest 5, 6, and 7.

The Oral Reading Sub-test reveals how fluid and expressive the child's reading is, and whether the child can successfully apply his or her decoding skills and word knowledge. Generally, I recommend beginning with the passage at the second grade level, although if a child had marked difficulty with the Informal Reading Skills Sub-test, you might want to start with the first grade passage. As the student reads the passage from the Student Passage Sheet, you follow along using the Oral Reading Student Record Sheet. Be sure to note any errors the child makes, writing them above the actual words on the sheet you are using, and write down any impressions you have about the child's reading. For guidelines about administering and interpreting this sub-test, please refer to pages 67-84.

The Silent Reading Sub-test is the only part of the evaluation to be administered to the entire class at the same time. I would recommend doing this early in the morning, when your students are most alert. Before you start, make sure your students each have two sharpened pencils, as well as books to read or an assignment to do if they finish early. Plan on it taking about half an hour, and if you notice any children rushing through it and just marking the boxes, be sure to note this, as it will be valuable information when you are correcting and interpreting the tests. Following are the reading levels of the passages:

Passage 1 - first grade
Passage 2 - second grade
Passage 3 - first half of third grade
Passage 4 - second half of third grade

Organizing And Working With Your Reading Groups

In third grade, reading groups organized around students' current ability and skill levels continue to provide the most efficient and productive means of meeting your students' needs. If you have three groups, for example, you are likely to find that for your most advanced readers decoding is no longer an issue. They can quickly learn any needed phonetic skills and now need to concentrate on developing more advanced reading comprehension skills. For your middle group, meanwhile, the decoding process is becoming increasingly easy, and the students' comprehension skills are developing. But, your emerging readers are still struggling to decode and are just beginning to do comprehension work.

With all these different ability levels and instructional needs within the same classroom, material that is just right for some students is likely to be too challenging or too boring for others. So, you want to create groups of students who are comfortable working on the same material at the same time. The optimum number of students in a group is five or six; eight is the maximum. If, because of your class size, you need to have four groups, each group will have to do more independent work while you are instructing one of the other groups. This becomes easier as the year progresses and your students become more proficient readers who can handle lengthier assignments.

The evaluation results give you the information you need to create groups which accommodate the students' different levels and needs. First, you'll want to consider the results of the oral and silent reading sub-tests you have administered. Usually, these results reveal which children will need the most help, because they had difficulty with both sub-tests. Not only will they probably need extended help strengthening their phonic skills, their sight vocabulary may also be weak. A few will need additional help in rhyming, as well. Place all these children in one reading group.

To decide who goes into your other reading groups, first look at the results of the oral reading sub-tests. Divide the students into a stronger group and a weaker group (assuming you'll have a total of three groups), and then check the results of the silent reading sub-tests to see if they are aligned with the oral reading scores. Many students do equally well on both sub-tests, which makes placing the students in an appropriate group easy.

In some cases, however, there is a discrepancy, in which case you'll find it helpful to review the results of other sub-tests. If a student did everything well except the oral reading, for example, your notes might reveal that he or she seemed nervous when asked to read aloud, and this affected the results. You may also find that a student who had a relatively poor reading comprehension score might have been a slow but accurate worker who did not finish the sub-test in the time allotted, or someone whose second grade teacher may not have taught specific reading comprehension skills, or someone who truly had trouble comprehending the material.

Determining the actual, underlying reason for a particular score is not always quick or easy, which is why keeping your reading groups fluid is so important. Over time, you may find it advisable to switch a child to a different group for academic or social reasons, so you should re-evaluate your reading group placements periodically with this in mind.

As in first and second grade (see pages 84-86), reading groups enable a teacher to provide more individualized instruction. This remains important in third grade, because third graders are more mature and tend to become more committed students if allowed to participate in determining their learning process. Many examples of this come to mind, but two in particular stand out.

Jorge was a lovely third grader who spoke fluent English, even though it was his second language. He usually spoke Portuguese at home, which was the only language his caregiver spoke. And, as an only son with three sisters, he clearly held a special place in his family and was used to being consulted about matters that pertained to him. When we first started working together, I asked Jorge to tell me if he didn't know what a word meant, but because he never asked, I soon realized that he didn't want to admit he didn't know something. I therefore started previewing vocabulary words with him, and he wrote each word on the front of an index card and put its definition on the back.

Jorge took the cards home to study with his mother, and using the five-check system (see page 53) he learned an impressive number of words by the end of the year. He was delighted that he could learn so many words in this way, and he became comfortable enough to tell me when he didn't know the meaning of a word. I was fortunate enough to have time to go over the cards with him, but if you don't, you can pair one of your stronger readers with a child who needs this kind of help. Together, they can look up words in a children's dictionary, which may also include a sentence containing the word. Third graders enjoy using their newly acquired dictionary skills, so both parties are likely to be happy.

Will, another third grader, was a visual learner with some auditory problems. His concerned teacher told me that even though he studied his spelling words, he could not seem to remember them and was failing her quizzes. When I questioned Will about his study habits, he explained that he just looked at the words, and then his mother asked him to spell them aloud. I explained that if he wrote the words, said the words, and heard the correct spelling, remembering the words would be easier for him. I suggested that he write each word five times, spelling it aloud as he wrote, and then close his eyes and try to see the word in his mind. After that, his mother could give him a written spelling test.

Will was reluctant to do this, so we agreed to wait one more week and see how he did on his next quiz. When he had the same problem again, he agreed to give my method a try, and the following week he "aced" the quiz. Of course, he was delighted with the results and continued with his new study habits.

Reading groups enable you to help your students achieve these sorts of breakthroughs, by providing daily opportunities for you to work with each student in a small group or individually. And, while you are working with one group of students in these ways, your other students can be working independently on the new skills and information they have learned during their daily session with you.

As explained in the preceding chapters, I recommend having an hour and a half of reading group time every morning. Assuming you have three groups, you can work with each group and its members for a half hour, which leaves an hour for the other students to do their independent work. In order for this approach to be effective, your students must have appropriate and varied assignments in their Learning Packets (see pages 142-149), as well as a clear idea of your expectations.

In addition to their assignments, your students will also need other options they can choose if they finish their assigned work early. This can include work on their writing, as well as their reading, or a combination of the two. On some days, you may just want your students to work on some practice sheets that will help them with their language, reading comprehension, or writing. At other times, you may want to choose from some of the following possibilities:

- Your students can write in their Story Notebooks or practice their paragraph writing (see pages 159-160). Third graders are likely to spend increasing amounts of time on their writing as the year progresses.

- You can encourage your students to write articles for a school newspaper or magazine. Especially when children have special interests, this can be an effective way to support their interests and their writing. A child who finds writing difficult can be paired with another child, and then they can take turns being the scribe.

- This can also serve as a "club time" when students read about special interests, which can be a particularly effective way to encourage reading. I have found that even my most reluctant readers pore over material about a favorite subject. There might be a video club in which children read video magazines and reviews, or a sports club in which students read articles from magazines like *Sports Illustrated for Kids* or a newspaper sports section. Just ask your students about their favorite subjects and then brainstorm related reading materials.

- Your students can use oral or silent reading activities to further develop their reading skills and work on reading comprehension. In particular, you want all your students to be able to:

1. Find the important details of a passage or story.

2. Sequence the events of a passage or story.

3. Identify the main idea or ideas.

4. Draw a conclusion from the material.

To accomplish these four goals, you can use commercial material (see the Resource Section) or make your own. Following are some additional ideas for creating your own materials, which can be customized to match your students' interests and needs:

- You can create your own questions to accompany copies of short weekly reader articles or workbook stories. This can include having your students identify and underline the topic sentence in a particular paragraph, which will help them determine what the main idea is. If the article does not contain topic sentences, you can have your students write in sentence form what they think the main idea is.

- You can also teach your students to draw their own conclusions from an article or short story, by asking them open-ended questions such as, "What did you learn?" or "What did you think was most important?" Students should answer in writing, using sentences, and any answer that makes sense and is based on the reading material should be acceptable. Usually, I also ask my students to underline the sentences that helped them come to their conclusions, after I have first shown them how to do this during reading group time.

At the beginning of the year, I would only ask students in a stronger reading group to work with longer stories from trade books in this way, but by spring some of your emerging readers will probably be able to do this, too. Two collections that provide enjoyable stories for this sort of work are *Tales for the Perfect Child* and *The Stories Julian Tells*.

Of all the possibilities for independent work during reading group time, my students' favorites are undoubtedly the educational games. Climb and Slide, Shoot to the Stars, Robert's Treasure, Memory, Indianapolis 500, and Slam Dunk (described in earlier chapters or the Resource Section) are popular and easy to make. The first five games can help students practice specific phonic sounds and rules, as well to review sight words, while Slam Dunk provides an effective and enjoyable way to review prefixes and suffixes.

Third graders also love playing a simple syllable game in which words are written on index cards that are then cut up into syllables. Each word should be written on two cards, which are cut up the same way but put in different containers, where they are mixed up with other cards. The goal of the game is to see which contestant(s) can make the most words in five minutes. Children can play in pairs or as teams, with one child serving as the time keeper. I also find that my students also enjoy making the game. A more complicated version can be created as your students' syllabification skills improve, and you can have students make their own individual games based on word lists you supply.

Not only do games such as this help to teach and reinforce important skills and information, they also provide a needed break during the daily hour and a half your students devote to reading. As the year progresses, however, most of your students will not need to play these games as much, so you may decide to substitute other relaxing reading activities. The suggestions made in the previous chapter (see page 85) can be just as applicable in third grade as they are in second grade.

As was also noted in the previous chapter, any available aides, parent volunteers, or older students can provide important support and supervision for the reading groups doing independent work while you are working with another group. And, because third graders are generally more mature and have more advanced reading skills, you can also organize more cooperative learning projects. In particular, pairing students who have different ability levels can provide weaker students with individualized attention and support, while the stronger students solidify their knowledge and develop important social skills.

Third Grade Learning Packets

In addition to the activities described above, your students should have Learning Packets that contain specific assignments and materials to work with during their independent reading group time. Knowing that third graders are becoming increasingly mature and developing longer attention spans, you can start including a greater variety of assignments and make them longer as the year progresses.

A typical Learning Packet should include phonics and language sheets, a composition book, each student's Story Notebook, an appropriate book for independent reading, reading skills books (that combine text and questions), and comprehension sheets. Also, additional handwriting practice sheets should be included for students who need them. Following are two sample Learning Packet assignments, which would be completed during the students' first half hour of independent work.

Use these words to complete the sentences below.

mouth couch clown ounce throw south blow
ground scoutmaster blouse cow clouds town row

1. Does the _____ make you laugh?

2. Birds go _____ in the winter.

3. The _____ broke when the boy jumped on it.

4. My dad said, "Don't talk with your _____ full."

5. Can the pitcher really _____ the ball that quickly?

6. Does an _____ make a pound?

7. Does the wind _____ in a storm?

8. The baby slipped and fell to the _____.

9. My sister got a new _____ for her birthday.

10. I think that my dad is a great _____ .

11. Every morning the farmer must get up and milk the _____.

12. At camp the children learn how to _____ a boat.

13. When there are black _____, it often rains.

14. I live in the country, but I am not far from _____.

To answer these riddles you must use a word that has
<u>ou</u> or <u>ow</u> in it.

1. The candy was not sweet. It was _____.

2. When my grandfather was unhappy, he often _____.

3. We grind wheat into _____.

4. The farmer used cheese to trap the _____.

5. I fish in the river and hope to catch a _____.

6. Water and sun make plants _____.

7. The opposite of high is _____.

8. In a storm the wind _____.

9. You have to be funny to be a circus _____.

10. The opposite of square is _____.

11. A baseball pitcher knows how to _____.

12. The opposite of north is _____.

VC/CV, V/CV or VC/V

Divide these words into syllables and write the rule that you used.

prin/cess <u>vc/cv</u>   ba/con <u>v/cv</u>   men/u <u>vc/v</u>

paper _____   connect _____   lemon _____

helmet _____   tulip _____   taffy _____

muffin _____   dentist _____   beside _____

radar _____   cabin _____   banner _____

liver _____   collar _____   bacon _____

tonsil _____   bonus _____   platform _____

talent _____   command _____   frozen _____

hotel _____   camel _____   trumpet _____

Syllabification

Divide these words into syllables and write the rule that you used.

com/ment <u>vc/cv</u>   be/long <u>v/cv</u>   wag/on <u>vc/v</u>

summer _____   circus _____   devil _____

open _____   clinic _____   coffee _____

prefer _____   wonder _____   solid _____

fever _____   polite _____   supper _____

Use the words above and fill in these sentences.

1. Did you _____ the door for your mother?

2. Did you dress as the _____ at Halloween?

3. The boy has a _____ and had to stay home from school.

4. Did you have spaghetti for _____?

5. Do you like _____ or tea?

6. The girl was sick, so her mother took her to the _____.

7. I _____ if my mother will like her birthday gift.

8. In the _____ I go to the beach.

9. It is not _____ to eat with your mouth full.

10. Do you _____ soccer or basketball?

11. I went with my family to see the _____.

12. Those rabbits are _____ chocolate.

Fall Learning Packet Assignment

In this first assignment, the child is reviewing (or learning) the diphthongs, *ou* and *ow*. As these diphthongs have just been introduced, the related practice sheets focus only on them. One sheet provides a list of words containing the diphthongs, followed by sentences containing a blank line where one of the words should go. Another sheet features a series of riddles, for which the answer is either an *ou* or *ow* word.

For further review, the children should write a paragraph using *ou* and *ow* words. At the top of the practice sheet, list the words that you want them to use, or provide a longer list and let each student choose five to use when writing. (If you think children may have trouble doing this individually, let them work in pairs.) At the end of the session, have the children read their paragraphs aloud. Each paragraph will be very distinct, and the children are likely to enjoy hearing what their classmates wrote.

Next, the children develop their silent reading comprehension skills by reading short passages with accompanying questions. For children who are reading at grade level, *Reading for Content, Book 1* is an excellent source for one-page nonfiction passages with main-idea and inference questions. *Reading About Science* is another popular book which contains a well-written series of passages with comprehension questions, starting at the second grade level. For children with weaker reading skills, I suggest using the *Specific Skills Series: Getting the Facts* and *Getting the Main Idea* (books A and B).

You can also assign some reading comprehension work from any workbooks you are having your students use. (I list a few appropriate ones in the Resource Section, and the reading specialist in your school may also be able to lend or recommend appropriate materials.) Once your students finish this work, they can read their independent reading books.

To vary the routine at this time of year, you can also have your students do some different activities, such as those listed on pages 153-154. Or, you can have your students practice a specific reading skill. For example, to teach sequencing skills you write a paragraph and follow it with a number of sentences that describe the events of the paragraph, but in a mixed-up order. Your students' assignment is to write a number next to each sentence, showing the actual sequence of the paragraph.

Spring Learning Packet Assignment

This assignment reviews syllabification rules for the following types of words: vowel consonant/consonant vowel, vowel/consonant vowel, and vowel consonant/vowel. The students start by using a practice sheet which lists these types of two-syllable words. The students use a slash to show where the words should be divided and then write which type of word it is next to the word (*sig/nal* - vc/cv). At the top of the next sheet are a number of words that the students divide into syllables. Then, they use the appropriate word from the top of the page to complete one of the sentences at the bottom of the page.

Next, the students do reading comprehension exercises. Usually, I start by assigning a set of three passages from one book, such as one of the books mentioned in the preceding section, which are still appropriate in the spring. I then try to vary the routine with a different type of reading comprehension exercise. One possibility is to provide a number of different paragraphs and ask your students to choose an appropriate title that expresses the main idea of each one. Or, your students can summarize the chapter or story they are reading during their reading group time. You can also have the children read the directions for a project such as making a paper whistle or an airplane, and then try to make it.

Once they have finished their reading comprehension work, the students read their in-dependent reading books and write a summary of the chapter they have read. In the summary, they must discuss the setting, plot, and order of events. This will help your students develop their reading comprehension skills, as well as their writing ability. (Make sure to review this sort of exercise with the whole class before assigning it for independent work, and remember that when students are doing this work, having aides, volunteers, older students, or peer tutors available can be very helpful.)

Knowing that your students will finish their work at different times, you'll want to have some other activities ready and waiting for them. Obviously, children who need additional practice in a particular area should be steered in that direction. For example, rather than just creating titles for some specific paragraphs, a student working on reading comprehension could create chapter titles for a favorite book which doesn't already have them. This provides terrific practice in summarizing the key events of a story.

For children who need further work on their writing skills, make a list of "kernel" sentences on a practice sheet. (He runs _____. She jumps _____.) At the top of the sheet, write the key *wh* words: *who, what, when, where, why.* Have the students use their imagination and some or all of the *wh* words to write expanded sentences. This can be done individually or in pairs, and when the assignment is complete, your students are likely to enjoy listening to each others' sentences and discussing how they are different.

Phonics & Whole Language—
An Integrated Approach

For many students third grade is the year that the act of reading becomes more auto-matic, and the process changes from pattern recognition to linguistic understanding. In other words, rather than focusing just on the phonetic aspects of decoding, students can also use context and meaning to help them with their reading. Continued work on phonics is needed for students to practice and consolidate their phonetic decoding skills, while their reading of a rich variety of literature supports their increasing understanding of the meaning of words.

Phonics Sequence For The Year

Following is the phonics sequence I recommend for third graders. This is a key year for phonics, because fourth graders are usually expected to have already mastered this work. Much of this material was probably introduced in second grade, so some students will need only a brief review before advancing further. Nevertheless, you should make sure the skills are automatic before allowing students to proceed to the next step, and you should also be prepared to have other students who will need months of review before they are ready to move on to new material.

1. Review of short vowels
2. Review of consonant digraphs *ch, th, sh, wh* (i.e., *chop, ship, this, whip*)
3. Review of initial and final consonant blends, starting with two letters and expanding to three letters (i.e., *step, pump, strip*)
4. Review of "magic *e*" rule, in which the *e* added at the end of a word makes the preceding vowel long (i.e., *lane, bride*)
5. Review of vowel digraphs, when two vowels go together, the first one says its name and the second one is silent (i.e., *dream*)
6. Word endings (*s, es, ing, est, y,* and *ed*—pronounced like a *t* as in *hoped*, a *d* as in *named*, and an *ed* as in *landed*)
7. Compound words
8. Hard and soft *c* and *g* (as pronounced in *cake, cent, gum, giraffe*)
9. Vowels before r (*er, ir, ur, ar, or*—notice that *e, i,* and *u* all have the same sound when followed by *r*)
10. Vowel digraphs and diphthongs (*oo, oi, oy, ou, ow, au, aw*—here two vowels go together, but make an entirely different sound than either one of them)
11. The prefixes *in, re, con, de,* etc.
12. The suffixes *ness, tion, ance, ful,* etc.
13. Syllabification using the following rules:

    A. Consonant-*le*—When a word ends in *le* and there is a consonant before it, the consonant goes with the *le* (i.e., *bat-tle, ri-fle,* etc.)

    B. Vowel-consonant/consonant-vowel rule—When there are two consonants between two vowels, syllable division is general between the two consonants (i.e., *ad-mit*). A syllable that ends with a consonant letter is a "closed" syllable, and a vowel within it will then have the "short" sound. A consonant blend counts as one consonant (i.e., *em-blem*).

    C. Vowel/consonant-vowel rule—When there is one consonant between two vowels, syllable division usually begins after the first consonant (i.e., *pu-pil*). In this v/cv pattern, the first syllable ends with a vowel and is an "open" syllable, so the vowel within it there has the "long" vowel sound (i.e., *ba* as in *baby*, *se* as in *select*, *pi* as in *pilot*, *so* as in *solo*, *hu* as in *human*).

D. Vowel-consonant/vowel rule—Some words are divided after the consonant letter (i.e., *rob-in*). In this vc/v pattern, the first syllable ends with a consonant letter and is a "closed" syllable, so the vowel letter therefore has a "short" sound (i.e., *rad* as in *radish*, *sev* as in *seven*, *liz* as in *lizard*, *com* as in *comic*, *pun* as in *punish*).

A key difference between learning this material in earlier grades and reviewing it in this grade is that when your students are ready, you can begin using more advanced words. For example, while reviewing the "magic *e*" rule, you use words such as *spade* and *throne* instead of *cone* and *pine*. And, fortunately, third graders love knowing long words, so they are often enthusiastic about learning syllabification.

All of this material is taught most efficiently during reading group time, when your students are grouped according to their skills. As in second grade, when you first introduce a new sound or rule, dictate eight words that incorporate the sound and then two sentences using words that contain the sound. During the days that follow, each group should have daily dictations which help them practice what they have learned. To vary the routine, on some days you can make the sentences open-ended and have the students complete them. Then, have the students read what they have written. On another day, you might dictate five silly sentences using words that contain the sound. Or, you might decide to use a short mystery (with your students as key figures) or a nonsense story (set in your students' neighborhood) as your phonics dictation.

These reading group lessons are important and challenging work, so I recommend scheduling them for the morning, when your students are most alert. The time of year in which you will introduce specific skills is much more variable. Your lowest-level reading group will need a lot of review before their knowledge of diphthongs becomes automatic, and they may not be ready to begin syllabification until fourth grade. Your middle and advanced groups will move at a faster rate, but you will still need to continuing presenting material in different ways to keep all your students interested.

In addition to using the techniques mentioned above, you can also tailor your lessons to a particular reading group by organizing them around interesting books that are challenging but still appropriate for the group. Carefully planning the type and amount of support you provide in regard to the books can make the lessons even more appropriate for a particular group. For example, with the weaker group you might have a detailed discussion about some preview questions before you ask them to read a chapter at school or at home. With the middle group, you might simply assign the chapter and have them answer accompanying questions for homework, and with your advanced group you might include some more inferential questions.

Sample Review Lesson for a Reading Group

Although the diphthong *oo* is taught in second grade, I find that many children need to review it in third grade, as well. I start this process by writing *oo* on the board along with two key words: *moon* and *book*. I draw the long vowel symbol over the *oo* in *moon* and pronounce the sound. Then, I ask my students to think of words that make that sound. Usually, the students can name a number of words, which I write on the board, but if they can't, I supply a few (*smooth, boost,* etc.). Next, I make the short vowel symbol over the *oo* in *book* and pronounce it, then ask for corresponding words that I also write down.

Children often have difficulty discriminating between the long and short sounds, so I divide the board into columns with *moon* at the top of one column and *book* at the top of the other. Then, I display a series of *oo* words on flash cards and write each one on the board, to the left of the two columns. (If you can find these words in a book that the group is reading, this process will probably be more meaningful for your students.) A volunteer reads each word and puts a checkmark in the appropriate column. The children then decide which words they want to use as their key words and write the words on cards they will keep in their Word Boxes.

Next, I dictate the following words and sentences:

Proof, mistook, swoop, gloom, smooth, backwoods, spook.

Do you boo hoo when you see a sad cartoon?

Can you use a spoon for a fishhook?

Then, I ask for a student volunteer who will think of a sentence using two other *oo* words and dictate it to the rest of the class. I might also write some more *oo* words on the board and ask all the students to write sentences using each one. Or, I might give the students some page numbers from a book they are reading and ask them to find the *oo* words on those pages.

After that, I introduce the new sight words from the chapter we are reading together. Sometimes, I ask the students to quickly preview the chapter themselves and see if there are any words they are not familiar with or don't know the meaning of. The chapters are then read aloud to the group (usually by the children, but sometimes I also participate) and followed by some comprehension questions. Often, I ask the children to underline the text in answer to the questions (after having practiced this skill). Or, for a change of pace, I might give the students a few minutes to create their own comprehension questions, which we then discuss together.

On other days, the chapter reading and written comprehension questions become homework assignments, after having been discussed during reading group time. The remaining group time is then spent on another reading comprehension activity. For example, I might act as the scribe while we all write a chapter summary together.

Sample Reading Group Lesson Introducing The VC/CV and V/CV Rules For Three-Syllable Words

These rules were initially taught in regard to two-syllable words, so I start this lesson by writing a few appropriate two-syllable words (i.e., *wan-der*) on the board. (If possible, select words from books the group members are currently reading.) I then ask for volunteers to come up and split the words, marking the vowels as open or closed and explaining what they did. Next, I turn to a list of three-syllable words on another part of the board, pointing out that words often have more than two syllables and may contain both vc/cv and v/cv syllables. I pronounce the first three-syllable word and divide it up (*ad-ver-tise*), using colored chalk and explaining which rules I used.

I also emphasize to the students that they always use the second vowel of the first split to help determine the second split. (In *e-las-tic*, the *a* is used in the first split as well as in the second split.) This is something that children often have trouble remembering, so they need to practice it.

After dividing a few more of these words and marking the vowels myself, I ask for volunteers to come to the board and go through the same process with some other words. Finally, I hand out sheets containing multi-syllabic words. Together, we split the first few words, and then the students must divide the rest of the words in the first column by themselves, while I walk around checking their work. Next, they do the second column, and I call on students to tell the group what each word is and why they split the word where they did. Once the students go through this experience, you can split the group into teams and make a game out of splitting and reading the words in the third column.

This work is followed by reading the next part of a chapter book, and then a comprehension assignment such as asking the students to write a paragraph describing their favorite scene in the chapter. They can also make a diorama or poster to accompany the paragraph. Another possibility is to have your students create a portrait of the character, comprised of a written and an artistic sketch. And, I have found that children love reading a book and then seeing a film version of the story. There are then a multitude of related writing assignments that can be based on comparing the book and the film.

Phonics Activities & Games

Most of the activities suggested for second graders and described in the preceding chapter (see pages 101-102) are just as appropriate for third graders. In particular, the following educational games—modified to focus on phonics—are enjoyable ways for third graders to practice their skills:

- Climb and Slide

- Memory

- Indy 500

- Robert's Treasure

- Slam Dunk

The Word Box (see page 53) also remains an indispensable tool. The Sound Book (see page 101), on the other hand, no longer appeals to all students. While many still find it useful, some third graders think that making a picture is too "babyish," so they prefer to write the words instead. If this works well, I would support it. When a student forgets a key word, however, I might explain that drawing a picture can be a better reminder.

Read! Read! Read!

One perceptive teacher calls third grade the year that children start reading for joy. To help make this come true for all your students, you need to make reading an integral part of the school day, provide a range of appropriate reading materials, and organize activities that support the reading process.

I recommend scheduling recreational reading time at least three days each week, as this helps reading become a habit. It also becomes something the children look forward to, if they know they will have interesting material that they can successfully read. In addition to new books, students should be encouraged to re-read favorite books, including "oldies but goodies" from when they were young. This can be an enjoyable activity that develops reading fluidity, and it can be expanded to include the students taping themselves reading stories and donating the tapes to a kindergarten or first grade class.

Along with books from their younger days, your students need plenty of books that reflect their growing maturity and interests. Just as third graders enjoy forming clubs with strict membership rules, they also enjoy reading about children dealing with various social situations. And, they relish stories about other children's adventures and escapades, which is why Louise Fitzhugh's *Harriet the Spy* and Beverly Cleary's *Henry and the Clubhouse* are such perennial favorites.

Joke books, mysteries, and adventure books are also popular items in third grade. And, most third graders love reading and listening to myths, as well as writing extensions of them or creating new ones. Third graders are also becoming more secure in their world and love reading about characters who go on remarkable journeys, including travel back and forth in time. *The Castle in the Attic* and *Half Magic* are two examples of this genre.

Proud of their developing verbal prowess, third graders love trading banter and are intrigued by word play. They enjoy reading books based on words that have double meanings, and while there are many such books available, my students always enjoy Fred Gwynne's *The King Who Rained* and the poetry of Ogden Nash.

A classroom library containing these sorts of books and other reading material becomes a vital resource for your students. Children often enjoy hearing the funny verses or the rich language of poems, so a few books of poetry should be available. Consider having appropriate works by Hilaire Belloc, Edward Lear, e.e. cummings, and Langston Hughes, to name just a few. There should also be a selection of children's magazines, such as *Sports Illustrated for Children* or the junior version of *National Geographic* (ask parents for donations). Interesting articles from old *Weekly Readers* can also be mounted and displayed.

In addition to providing a variety of reading materials, you need to make sure your library provides materials at a variety of reading levels. Materials that children can enjoy and read relatively quickly and easily inspire them to keep reading. And, children who have reading difficulties are often very sensitive about choosing books, so it's helpful to have a wide selection of easier books available. Yet, you also need more challenging materials that stimulate and support continued growth.

An example of this would be the chapter books that can be used for silent reading as part of specific group assignments, and remain in the classroom library, as well. At the beginning of the school year, and especially with weaker readers, the chapter books I introduce are relatively short. Two popular examples would be *Chocolate Fever* and *Aliens for Breakfast*. In the latter part of the year, most students have moved on to longer books, such as the wonderful classic, *Charlotte's Web*.

Students also need to find a diversity of topics that match different interests and support continued reading. For example, a book about airplanes might lead to further reading about the Wright brothers or Amelia Earhart. This has become especially important now that so many children no longer read content-related stories at home. You have to fill in the gaps by expanding students' horizons and knowledge, as well as providing entertaining books. Fortunately, many third graders enjoy reading general information books and biographies, which should also be readily available in the classroom library.

Of course, many parents also don't read aloud to their children, so you must also try to make up for this lack of language enrichment. Reading aloud to your class during a regularly scheduled story time is just as important in third grade as it was in earlier grades. Hearing an interesting story encourages children to read and serves as an effective means of language development. First, of course, you should introduce the book, matching the extent of your introduction to the complexity of the story. I find that children with reading and/or auditory problems find an introduction of the characters and setting very helpful.

Discussions about books are another type of supportive experience that now occur rarely, if at all, in many homes. This increases the importance of the discussions you lead about reading material. In addition to talking about books the class has read, I recommend bringing in newspaper and magazine articles that you think your students would find interesting. In my city, for example, there are plans to tear down the existing children's zoo and replace it with a new one, and after I read aloud an article about the plans, almost all my students wanted to express their opinions, because they had been to the zoo. This sort of discussion can easily lead to additional reading and/or writing projects, as well as the opinion polls and bar graphs that many third graders love.

Rather than just accepting the lack of modeling at home, however, encourage parents to read and discuss books and other material with their children, in addition to supporting the reading process in other ways. You may want to send a letter home that recommends a range of supportive activities and explains that reading is like playing a musical instrument—it takes practice. Not only should students read for twenty minutes every day as part of their homework, they can keep a journal listing books they have read and describing their reactions to the books. Parents should also be taking children to the local library on a regular basis, and if necessary, you may want to schedule a class trip to the library, so everyone can get a library card.

You also want to show your class that reading is an integral part of your life. Knowing that television has replaced reading as a recreational activity in many homes, you need to demonstrate your enthusiasm and commitment to reading. In addition to bringing in interesting articles, from time to time to you can report on what you are reading at home. Don't underestimate the power of patterning!

Another effective way to promote reading is to establish reading partnerships. Ideally, third graders should have a partnership with students in a younger grade, as third graders usually grow very proud when they become older buddies for a kindergarten or first grade class. They love reading to the younger students and willingly practice the books that are chosen. And, I'm sure you can imagine how happy your third graders would be to receive thank-you notes with pictures on them, or to be invited to a thank-you party.

Oral Reading

Oral reading should continue in third grade, because it gives students hefty rations of the decoding and word recognition practice that helps them become fluent readers. It also helps them realize how important word analysis is. And, of course, an important bonus is that children enjoy reading a story together.

To make oral reading as productive as possible, be sure to participate in the oral reading with each group, keeping in mind that your voice is your students' model for correct pronunciation. At the same time, don't be afraid to play the part of characters in a story. Changing your voice to fit a role makes oral reading much more interesting, and your students are then likely to follow suit. A final reason for you to participate is that it quickens the pace.

Knowing that oral reading is required prompts some students to work harder on their decoding skills. No matter how proficient a student is, however, reading aloud to peers can be a nerve-wracking experience. Even in third grade, a child may complain that a dry mouth is interfering with his or her ability to read, in which case you may decide to let the child have a cup of water. It may be a crutch, but it can help a dry mouth, as well as any underlying stress, and it will rarely be requested throughout the year.

To further alleviate stress and to develop all your students' reading skills, I would recommend using the following procedures (which are described in more detail in the previous chapter) before oral reading:

1. Preview the text with your students. Be sure to discuss any words that are likely to be difficult for them.

2. If a child hesitates for a few seconds, say the word.

3. If a child makes a mistake, don't focus on the error, but do say the correct word.

4. Disregard unimportant errors, such as repeating a word or omitting an ending like *ed*.

If possible, review any important errors after the child finishes reading. For example, if a child substitutes a word that is similar in meaning (i.e., *beautiful/pretty*), write the word from the text on the board and ask the child to say it. If the child hesitates for a few seconds, say the word and be sure to praise the child for understanding the word's meaning.

Another common error is substituting a similar-looking word (i.e., *crashed/crushed*). In this situation, help the child to read *crash* and then *crashed*. Be sure to compliment the child if he or she uses an effective decoding strategy, as the compliment will make the child more aware of how important and useful this sort of strategy is.

Reading Comprehension

The reading comprehension techniques introduced in second grade—discussion, patterning, and previewing the characters and plot (see pages 105-106)—become even more important in third grade, when the goal for students becomes learning how to obtain information from a text by themselves. As the year unfolds and the students develop these vital reading skills, they also develop more competence and confidence, and so can do more independent reading.

To support this process, I start working with third graders on reading comprehension right from the start of the school year. When we read a trade book aloud, I write guide questions (Why did this happen?) on the chalkboard and discuss them briefly before the group begins reading. Once we finish reading, I ask students to answer the questions, and as a patterning technique I repeat the child's answer but expand on it, making sure it is grammatically correct.

During the year, I often ask students to write the answers to these sorts of questions, after having first answered an initial question with a complete written sentence on the board. The students then write their answers to the other questions, while I walk around providing help when it is needed.

I recommend using a variety of trade books for reading comprehension work, devising different types of questions based on the text and saving them for use in the years that follow. For "at-risk" readers, matching reading material to their interests or prior knowledge, as well as their current ability level, is especially important. Not only does this encourage these students to read, it makes them more willing to do accompanying comprehension work, which can then be extended into related activities. And, as these students find that reading is providing them with enjoyment and information, it's a great morale booster for them.

In addition to working with trade books, I also use short paragraphs to introduce and develop reading comprehension skills during reading group time. At first, I have the students read the paragraphs aloud, but as they succeed with these exercises I have them read the paragraphs silently, and I gradually increase the length of the passages as the year progresses. Written questions and answers then follow.

Another effective technique, especially at the beginning of the year, is to write a few passages and accompanying questions on the board, with key words underlined in colored chalk, which is especially helpful for children who have difficulty focusing. A student volunteer reads the passage and the questions, and I then supply the answers, explaining how I approached each question and determined my answer.

Overall, third graders should become more active and independent partners in developing their reading comprehension skills. Here are a few examples of how this can happen:

1. Instead of using class time to introduce difficult words before reading a chapter, have the students read the chapter independently—either in school or as homework—and underline words that were difficult for them. Then, have the children discuss these words with the teacher during their reading group time.

2. Make reading a chapter and answering comprehension questions independently part of the reading routine.

3. Have your students read a chapter at home and underline a sentence that they think is important. The next day, have them explain why they chose their particular sentence. This makes them think about the chapter's meaning and purpose, and as the year progresses, their explanations should become more clear and concise.

4. As a homework assignment, have your students make a list of important quotes from a chapter. Then, on the following day let them see whether their classmates know who said each quote and why it was important.

Spelling

Spelling remains a critical component of a balanced reading program in third grade. Much of what needs to be done continues the work described in the preceding chapter on second grade (see pages 106-108), but the following are some important differences:

1. Begin working with the *Dolch List* on spelling sight words, and then choose a third grade spelling list.

2. Many of your third graders no longer need to use the kinesthetic method of learning sight words. Rather than having them trace the letters with their fingers, now encourage them to make pictures in their mind of a spelling word.

3. In addition to reviewing the spelling rules taught in second grade, introduce the Y Rule: When a word ends in y and has a vowel before the y, just add an s to form the plural (*boy, boys*). If there's a consonant before the y, drop the y and add *ies* (*lady, ladies*).

4. Third graders often remain unsure of the sound/symbol correspondence for short vowels (*fan, bed, pig, hot, sub*), so review these vowel sounds throughout the year.

5. Teach "chunking." Spelling becomes a much easier task when children are familiar with and know how to spell frequently encountered parts of words (*ing, ed, ful, pre, non, ed*, etc.).

Writing In Third Grade

The preceding chapter explains the basics of a writing program that starts in second grade and can continue through third grade (see pages 108-112). One important difference for proficient third graders has to do with paragraph writing, as a good number of your students will probably not need to spend much time on the preliminary steps. In fact, some students should be able to start the school year writing basic paragraphs with a topic sentence, supporting sentences, and a concluding sentence. A few students may be able to write expanded paragraphs where they elaborate further about their ideas.

Third graders should learn to write the expository paragraphs (explaining something) that they will be expected to do in the years ahead. Following are the three key types of expository paragraphs:

1. A basic *example* paragraph provides examples of something, with each supporting sentence offering a different example.

2. A *reason* paragraph provides reasons for something, such as Why I Enjoyed This Book.

3. A *process* explains how to do something step-by-step.

And, here's a suggestion for creative writing: third graders love learning the Greek myths, so a popular writing assignment is to have the students write extensions of their favorite myths—or create their own myths.

Third grade is also a time when students who are having difficulty with handwriting should do additional practicing. Some third graders still get cramps in their hands when they write, and these children need to strengthen their finger and hand muscles. One way to do this is with exercise putty (see the Resource Section), which helps with a hand-strengthening exercise routine. Doing these exercises for five minutes a day can be enjoyable and very effective, and third graders who need help with handwriting are usually willing to do this.

Language Development

As with writing, the general guidelines for developing second graders' language skills remain the same in third grade. However, the following new additions are important for third graders:

• Talk about homophones and lead brainstorming sessions during which your students see how many they can think of. Make a large homophone scroll and display it in your classroom, encouraging students to add new homophone pairs as they think of them. Write homophone riddles on the board (i.e., it is a place for planes, and it is used for hanging clothes), and then ask volunteers to come up and write the appropriate answers. You can also give each child a set of these word riddles on paper, and have the students work on them together (this is a wonderful time for mixed grouping). And, be sure to play word games and share jokes that depend on word play.

• After a quick review of similes (see pages 114-115), introduce metaphors to your class. Headlines from the sports section of a local newspaper are often a good source of metaphors that capture students' attention and interest. It can be fun to have your students copy some of these headlines onto pieces of drawing paper and create a class metaphor book. Or, you can create a metaphor contest, in which the class is divided into teams which race to find a certain number of metaphors in a book of prose or poetry.

• Third grade is often the year in which dictionary skills are introduced, and to help children practice these new skills, divide your class into pairs and assign them different words to look up. Then, have them report the various word meanings to their classmates and make up sentences using the words. When your students become proficient in using the dictionary, make this into a game by setting up teams and having them race to look up and use a list of words.

One savvy third grade teacher uses third graders' interest in geography to help them practice their dictionary skills. She keeps a large map of the world on a wall and has her students look up words related to different places (*Tunisia* and *sari*) are two examples. When students find the word, they write down the definition and stick in a colored pin in the appropriate country. In this way, an interesting activity helps third graders strengthen their dictionary and geography skills at the same time.

• In addition to using variety in your own language, expose children to the richness of words by introducing proverbs, idioms, and figures of speech. When I first introduce proverbs and provide some examples, I often see blank expressions on some students' faces. (One daughter of two successful professionals told me, "In our house, we never talk that way.") I find, though, that children enjoy learning new proverbs after a while, and parents tell me that their children quiz them about proverbs learned at school.

To support this work, you can have a "proverb of the week" spot on your bulletin board, where the proverb is accompanied by a student's illustration. Of course, you can do this for idioms and figures of speech, too. And, creating a flip book of proverbs can also be an enjoyable and educational activity. Each student can use a spiral notebook, in which he or she writes a proverb at the top of the page and then underneath draws a picture depicting it. Have the students compare their work and see how their pictures differ.

Developing Auditory Skills

In third grade, the development of auditory skills continues along the same lines described in the previous chapter (see pages 116-117), but at more challenging levels. One important new activity is to have your students listen to stories on tapes and then answer written comprehension questions. They can also listen to stories on tapes and then write summaries of them. These activities can be done by students working in groups, who then discuss their work together, or this can be an individual assignment.

To support this process, encourage your students to make mental pictures of what they are hearing, and show them how making a small rebus can help them remember important information. And, as in past years, playing the games "In Grandmother's Trunk" and "At the Supermarket I Bought..." can continue to strengthen auditory memories in an enjoyable way.

To succeed in the grades that follow, third graders should be able to obtain information and pleasure from their reading. This, in turn, requires them to have strong decoding skills, a large sight vocabulary base, and a strong language sense. The integrated approach described in this chapter should provide your students with this needed base for future success.

CHAPTER 6

Teaching Students Who Have Special Needs

Most of the teaching strategies and materials described in the previous three chapters work well for students who have special needs. These students need to learn the same basic phonics skills and find reading enjoyable and interesting. In order for this to happen, however, I often have to modify the approach I use so that it meets the specific needs of the student. When I give a phonics assignment to a child who has A.D.D., for example, I break the assignment into smaller segments and try to give the child quick feedback. And, when I work with an E.S.L. child, I make sure to supplement phonetic instruction with healthy doses of sight words.

The following sections of this chapter explain the range of techniques I have found successful in teaching reading to numerous children who have the types of special needs now found in many classrooms. While I believe this information will prove helpful in working with these specific sorts of children, I also recognize that meeting these children's needs, as well as the needs of the rest of your class, often requires tremendous effort, detailed planning, and some outside assistance. As a classroom teacher, you alone simply cannot be there for each child every time they want your help. So, you need a strong support system that extends throughout your school and community.

As noted in the preceding chapters, you'll want to make good use of any available aides, parent volunteers, and older students. Senior citizens or other members of your community may also be available to spend time in your classroom, allowing you to spend more time working with individual children. Even so, you may also need to have peer tutors help by responding to questions and checking answers. And, of course, for more specialized help in meeting special needs, you should also have your school or district reading specialist and psychologist working closely with you. Help may also be available through The Orton Dyslexia Society, Children with Attention Deficit Disorders (CHADD), or a local teachers' college.

Whatever the situation in your school or community, the ultimate responsibility for teaching your students to read still rests with you, and the following information can help some of your most challenging students to become successful and enthusiastic readers.

Working With E.S.L. Students

Many classroom teachers are now responsible for teaching children whose primary language is not English. Often, these students have lived in the United States for years and can speak English well, but we know that English is rarely spoken at home. These students are likely to need additional help perfecting their English usage and developing their vocabulary and reading skills.

Other E.S.L. students have only recently arrived in the United States, and they may speak and read virtually no English. In the past, these children were usually placed in special E.S.L. classrooms or at least received additional instruction from an E.S.L. specialist. Now, however, these students may be "mainstreamed" in a regular classroom, with or without support from a specialist. Either way, they are likely to need individualized instruction and support from their classroom teacher in order to read English successfully and with pleasure.

Over the years, I have been fortunate to work with many E.S.L. students and come to know their families well. These experiences have confirmed for me that the two major elements of a balanced approach to reading instruction are especially important for these students: they need to develop the range of age-appropriate phonics and other skills that will enable them to read, and through reading they need to be able to explore topics that interest them, whether sports, magic tricks, or "knock knock" jokes they can tell to their friends.

In addition, these students must also feel comfortable and secure in their classroom, so that they can focus on the challenges they face and not be overly concerned about making the mistakes that are an inevitable part of the learning process. With this in mind, here are few suggestions for helping an E.S.L. student adjust to your classroom environment:

1. A good way to get to know E.S.L. students and build a basis for regular communication is to ask about their family and talk about yours. E.S.L. students are usually delighted to tell you about their family members, so I try to find out the names and interests of siblings, and then I often ask about them by name.

2. Learning a few key words in a student's native language can be very useful and help put the child at ease.

3. Make signs for important classroom objects in English and in a student's native language. This helps them learn English words and shows that you think their language is important.

4. Establish a "buddy" system for an E.S.L. child. Of course, the first step is to find a willing volunteer and explain separately to each child what his or her responsibilities are.

5. As soon as possible, find opportunities to praise E.S.L. students and let them know you are delighted to have them in your classroom. Many E.S.L. parents have told me that early praise for their children's work and/or behavior made the children feel they were successful members of the class.

Reading & Writing Instruction For E.S.L. Students

Along with the five suggestions listed above, there are a number of language-oriented techniques you can use to prepare E.S.L. students for reading English. Of course, one of the most important is your serving as an appropriate model whenever you read or speak to your students. Following are some additional steps that I have found particularly helpful:

- **Theme-Oriented Stories** - Reading and writing stories related to a theme is an effective and wonderful way to expand students' English vocabulary. If you decide to base a theme on zoos, for example, you and/or your students can bring in pictures of various animals and objects that you might find at a zoo. You can then have your students dictate a zoo-related story that includes some of the animals and objects pictured. Or, depending on your students' abilities, you can write the first line and have your students complete the story. Once it is finished, you can all read the story together. And, using a colored marker, you can underline some key words in the story and ask your students to pick out the picture that goes with each word.

The story and pictures can also be used to practice language skills in a variety of ways. As a warm-up activity during your language arts time, you can quickly review the picture cards and ask students if they know how to say the English word for each one. When you think your students are ready to learn some sight words, you can write some of the words on large flash cards and ask your students to match each card to an underlined word in the story. You can review the words daily until you think they are automatic, and as part of this process you may want to add the words to your students' Word Card Boxes (see page 53). Even after all this has been done, you may want to keep the story available in your classroom and periodically ask your students if they remember some of the key words.

- **Language Experience Stories** - A teacher I know took a class of second graders, who were mostly Spanish-speaking, on a trip on a ferry. She was careful to explain that they were going on a "boat" and mentioned the word several times when they were traveling on the ferry. Then, while they were still on the ferry, one of her students pointed to a helicopter flying overhead and said, "Look, a boat."

This is when a class trip can be so educational for a teacher, as well as the students. In this case, it led the teacher to have the whole class work on a thematic unit about transportation, which included language experience stories.

When you first have students develop these sorts of stories, guide them into retelling their experiences in an organized, sequential way. For example, you might want to write the first sentence and then have the students recount all the major events—in response to your questions. As the story develops, introduce key vocabulary words and ask the students if they know the words' meanings. Students who have difficulty should have the words explained to them and then should review the words periodically. You might even want to make a poster of interesting new words related to the experience.

- **Cooking** - Cooking can be an enjoyable way to introduce and practice new vocabulary words as part of a small group or whole class activity. Just think of all the new words children can learn while making a simple recipe. And, because the children are actually doing the cooking, the experience itself helps them remember the words. Of course, this is also a great time to have parent volunteers help.

- **The Word Card Box** - In addition to the uses of this box described earlier (see page 53), it can also be adapted to meet some of the special needs of E.S.L. students. For example, knowing that children learn words more easily if related words are taught together, you may decide to teach the names for various pieces of furniture or items found in a kitchen. You can start by gathering pictures from a store catalog or from *Sparc*, a language book that has pictures grouped by category. Then, you meet with a group of children, show a card, say what it is, and have the children repeat the word. Next, you use the word in a sentence and ask for a volunteer who can create a new sentence with the word in it. The students complete this phase of the activity by stapling the pictures to index cards, which then have the word written on the back of the card. The cards go in the students' Word Card boxes.

Once you have established this procedure, work with additional categories of words could be led and supervised by an aide, parent volunteer, or older student. Another possibility is pairing an E.S.L. student with an English-speaking classmate.

Sometimes, you may not have pictures handy for words you want to teach. When this happens, I just draw a sample picture and then ask the students to draw their own pictures. Although these pictures sometimes seem to bear little resemblance to the object being discussed, the children remember what they represent, which is, of course, the purpose of the exercise. As with other words on the language cards, these pictures should be reviewed until the child can remember the word five times in a row and so receives five checks on the card. After that, many children do not need any additional review of the words, so you have to use your judgment as to whether to go over them again from time to time.

This technique can also be used to teach verbs, tenses, antonyms, synonyms, and word associations (*baseball/bat*). And, as you work with E.S.L. students in this way, you may find that many of your English-speaking students would also benefit from this type of work, which could become a project for a group or even a whole class.

- **Games** - As with English-speaking students, I have found that games are great teaching tool for E.S.L. students. Using your own pictures and/or words, you can make a variety of games, including a category game (colors, animals, transportation, clothing, etc.), an antonym game, a concentration game, and a picture-based version of Climb and Slide (see page 51 and the Resource Section). Initially, I recommend having one of your English-speaking students play, too, because the E.S.L. students may need help with English words. These sorts of educational games are popular activities during choice time, and as your E.S.L. students learn to read English, they will benefit greatly from the reading and language games recommended in Chapters 3 through 5, as well.

When teaching E.S.L. students to read English, I used a two-pronged approach that introduces the students to phonics and uses the sight method, too. The way in which this is done depends on the make-up of the class. If there are enough E.S.L. students in the class at the same reading level, and that level is appreciably lower than that of your other students, you may decide to form a fourth reading group (see pages 33-34 for information about working with a fourth reading group) until the members are ready to be integrated into your other reading groups.

If you have only a few E.S.L. students whose skills are lower than your other students, you can make them members of the lowest-level reading group. These E.S.L. students may need preliminary phonics and sight word work that the other members do not need to do, in which case the best solution is to have an aide or parent volunteer provide additional help individually or to a small group. Otherwise, you might be able to arrange for an older student to help them, or you can set up a cooperative learning plan in which they review their work with classmates every week.

When E.S.L. students are in the lowest reading group, you'll want to make sure to incorporate the following teaching techniques into the reading group's program, which will also benefit the English-speaking group members:

1. **Sound/symbol correspondence** - Begin with the initial and final consonant sounds (remembering that some sounds are not the same in other languages) and progress from there, based on the teaching order for phonics described in Chapters 3-5.

2. **Blending** - Begin with the auditory blending of interesting, multi-syllabic words (*won-der-ful*) and then introduce the c-v-c words.

3. **Auditory Discrimination** - To help develop syllable awareness, start with auditory discrimination of the initial and final sounds (Do you hear the *mis* in *mistake*? Do you hear the *phone* in *telephone*?) and then work with medial sounds (Do you hear the *der* in *wonderful*?).

4. **Sight Words** - Write a word on the front of an index card and put or draw a corresponding picture on the back. Have the student dictate a sentence that includes the word, which you write under the picture. At the beginning of each session, review words prepared in this way, because frequently seeing the words helps children internalize them. The review process consists of showing the word and asking for a volunteer to read it. If there are no volunteers, say the word and then show the picture on the back of the card. Depending on the reading level of the group, you can also ask for a volunteer to read the sentence under the picture, or you can read it. Next, ask who can make up a sentence using the word. You can reinforce students' recognition of these words by writing sentences that contain the words on the chalkboard, and by using these words as part of the sight word games described on pages 141-142.

5. **Review, Review, Review** - Sight words and sound/symbol correspondence should be reviewed again and again, until they become automatic.

To support E.S.L. students' listening, speaking, and writing, continue using theme-oriented work that helps the students develop their thoughts and vocabulary. This can be done as a class project lasting a week or more. For example, if your students are studying the ocean, they can write stories about the ocean and learn relevant sight words. Music and art lessons that relate back to the ocean also help to reinforce the vocabulary and concepts introduced during a reading group lesson.

Working With Dyslexic Students

Due to budget cuts, parental requests, and recent legislation, increasing numbers of students who have dyslexia are being taught in "mainstream" classrooms, even though many of the "mainstream" classroom teachers were never taught how to work with children who have this learning disability. And, even teachers who did receive training are now likely to be in need of an update, because important new information is frequently becoming available about dyslexic students and the techniques that meet their special needs.

Meanwhile, experts continue to debate exactly what dyslexia is. The term comes from two Greek words: *dys*, which means "poor" or "inadequate," and *lexia*, which means "words." Basically, dyslexia is a specific learning disability characterized by difficulty learning to read, although some dyslexic students also have difficulty learning to write, spell, speak, or work with numbers. The Orton Dyslexia Society describes dyslexic people in the following way:

"Their problems in language processing distinguish them as a group. This means that the dyslexic has problems translating language to thought (as in listening or reading) or in translating thought into language (as in writing or speaking)."

Dyslexia is not a disease and does not have a cure. It is a result of differences in the structure and function of the brain. As with other learning disabilities, it needs to be evaluated and diagnosed by a professional, so the term should not be used in regard to children who have not been officially identified as having dyslexia. The following suggestions are techniques that I have found to be effective in working with children who have been identified as dyslexic. (Of course, some of these techniques may also prove helpful with other students having difficulty with language processing.)

Reading & Writing Instruction For Dyslexic Students

What is the overall instructional plan for your dyslexic students? There are a variety of factors and goals to consider. First and foremost, of course, you need to observe and evaluate each child individually and develop a plan based on the child's specific needs. Then, of course, you want each student to progress to the point at which he or she can read at grade level, but in reality this simply may not be possible.

Often, dyslexic students will need to be in your lowest-level reading group, and they need to feel secure in this group, as this will make them more attentive and enthusiastic. To help them succeed, you need to continually evaluate reading material to make sure it is appropriate for these students' reading level, and you need to systematically review what you have previously taught. In addition, dyslexic students may need to spend extra time reviewing new material that you introduce during their reading group time.

However, remain alert to the possibility that a dyslexic may be ready for a different reading group. If students were diagnosed and received good remediation before entering your class, their reading skills may be strong enough for them to succeed in a middle-level reading group. Another possibility is that sometime during the year, the child's skills may improve to the point where placement in a new group is appropriate.

Following are some additional recommendations for helping dyslexic students. Remember when reviewing these recommendations that it would be impossible to adopt them all at one time. Instead, just pick a few at a time to add to your teaching program, and then see how they work with specific students. Also, while the first few items may seem obvious, they are so crucial I feel it would be inappropriate to omit them.

- Praise and encouragement are especially important for dyslexic students. Reading and other forms of language development are not easy for these children, so your support and positive comments are needed to help them persevere.

- Make sure to show dyslexic students the specific gains they have made. For example, if a child is having more success answering comprehension questions, say something such as, "You are doing much better at answering questions about the main idea."

- As much as possible, remain non-judgmental. If a dyslexic student says, "I hate reading," you can simply say in a reflective voice, "I'm sorry to hear that," and then continue working.

- Techniques like those just listed will help you establish rapport with dyslexic students, which they need in order to achieve success. When dyslexic students like and trust you, they will be much more willing to risk embarrassment and failure and to "go the extra mile."

- Be prepared to repeat what you have already said or taught, but try to restate it in a different way so it does not bore or "turn off" the students. I sometimes explain, "It's my job to teach you, and it's up to me to think of a way that will make it possible for you to remember."

- Teach in a highly structured and organized way so that a dyslexic student moves step-by-step from simple to more complex material. With paragraph writing, for example, begin with simple listing and gradually introduce other needed skills. Remember not to go to the next level until the student has demonstrated that he or she can successfully handle work at the current level. And, if a child is having difficulty at a particular level, present the material in a different way.

- Make your instructions simple and effective. When giving oral directions, for example, it is extremely important to get the student's attention first, perhaps by quietly saying the child's name. You may then want to reinforce your oral directions by writing them on the chalkboard. And, when you use written directions, make sure a dyslexic student can read all the words, so he or she will know what to do. You may need to read the directions aloud or have another student do so. Using a rebus might also help with more difficult words.

- Be consistent in your approach. If you use *ouch* as the key word for the *ou* sound, changing to another key word later is likely to confuse a dyslexic student. Some dyslexics learn these words sounds automatically and do not need a key word, but for those who do, consistency is crucial.

- Over-teach: explain to your students why they must learn each step thoroughly before proceeding to the next step. Explain that they may forget a word or rule, but with continued review they will eventually learn it.

- Repeat, repeat, repeat. Always review what you taught yesterday, and periodically review older materials. If you are teaching the "magic *e*" rule, for example, and are now concentrating on the "magic *e*" with the vowel *o*, review the other long vowels you have previously covered.

- Use a multi-sensory approach, including kinesthetic activities. When children use as many modalities as possible, they become "saturated" with the material and are more likely to retain it.

- Individualize as much as possible. Of course, this can be difficult in a large class, but little actions can make a big difference. For example, if a dyslexic student is a sport fanatic, try to find sports stories at the appropriate reading level. Pair the child with a stronger reader who also loves sports, and together they can read an article or look for interesting statistics about players. The dyslexic student can also try to read a sports book along with an audiotape of the book. And, as "sports editor" of the class for a week, let the child write scores of school or professional sporting events on a sports scoreboard.

- Help dyslexic students develop an awareness of the types of errors they are prone to make, and teach them the importance of checking and then correcting their own work. When you discuss writing and spelling with your class as a whole, discuss the importance of this procedure for everyone and mention that all sorts of people often make these sorts of errors. I tell my students that I always check the letters and reports I write. I also find it very effective to write a few common errors on the board and point out the ones that I sometimes make. This helps students understand that everyone—even the teacher—is vulnerable and has to proofread.

- Compensate for each symptom of dyslexia by providing additional instruction and practice for that area. If a child has difficulty encoding, for example, spend extra time on it with the child and then give more practice assignments in a variety of formats that require encoding. If a child has difficulty distinguishing *b* from *d*, tape a card with the letter *b* on their desk. Form the letter by making a bat and ball and tell the child that both a bat and a ball begin with the letter *b*. If a student has difficulty distinguishing left from right, have the child wear a rubber band on the wrist that he or she uses when writing. When students have trouble setting up their writing papers, use a red pen to draw a line down the left-hand margin, and tell them this is where they begin writing a word or sentence. With older and less disabled students, you can simply put a green dot (for *go*) on the top left hand corner of the page, and tell them that this shows where to begin.

- Also compensate for areas of weakness by making greater use of dyslexic students' strengths. If a student has difficulty reading but is a great artist, have the child illustrate the class newspaper and help classmates with their drawing projects.

- In some situations, you should not require dyslexic students to read aloud unless you have previewed the material with them or they volunteer to read. For example, when a child has great difficulty decoding and is sensitive about this, reading in front of peers can be traumatic.

- When you and your class first begin reading longer chapter books aloud, showing a film version of the story can help dyslexics and other students who might have difficulty following the story line. Obviously, there is not a film version of every book, and you would not want to do this with every story anyhow, but many classic stories have been filmed and are available through your school or local library.

When appropriate, you could also suggest to a dyslexic child's parents that they borrow or rent the film, so as to help the child understand as well as enjoy the book.

- Make full use of audiotaped books when dyslexic students are having difficulty reading a book. You can make the audiotapes yourself or have an aide, parent, or other student do so. Dyslexic students can then listen to the tapes at school or at home, and—when capable enough—read the book along with the tape. Emphasize to the students that the tapes are a wonderful learning tool and should be played as often as needed. Also, point out that the students will find it helpful to stop the tape at times and think about what they have heard. If a few children are having trouble with the same book, you may be able to arrange a listening set-up that enables all of them to listen and read at the same time.

- Where possible, individualize testing procedures to allow dyslexic students to demonstrate what they have learned. For example, knowing that dyslexic students often write more slowly and may have trouble composing an answer, you want to allow them to answer some questions orally or have an extra time to answer. You may also want to simplify some questions, or read them aloud in person or on tape.

Some dyslexic students have "auditory dyslexia," which means they have difficulty processing information that is presented orally. With these students, I have found the following techniques helpful:

- Be sure to establish eye contact before talking to a student who has auditory dyslexia. Then, talk slowly, but not too slowly.

- Explain new material in very simple language and be prepared to repeat what you have said. When appropriate, you may also want to present new material with words, pictures, and symbols.

- Give one or two directions at a time, and then ask the child to repeat what you have said. (During a class activity, you may want to use a buddy system, in which another student is asked questions or listens while the directions are repeated, rather than calling only on a child who has difficulty processing oral directions.)

- Teach blending skills until they are automatic and teach segmenting skills until they are secure. Also teach vocabulary, and review new words again and again. Remember that these students are not always processing what they hear.

- Do exercises that help these students practice and increase auditory comprehension. For example, you can tape a short paragraph or story with accompanying comprehension questions from a workbook, or tape a set of drawing directions.

In addition to working specifically on reading and other aspects of language development, you should also be prepared to provide other forms of support that can help dyslexic students function more effectively in your classroom. Many students who have learning disabilities develop social, emotional, and family problems due to the frustrations and failures they experience, so you need to be prepared and understanding when these problems emerge in the classroom. This is especially true for the 20% to 25% of learning disabled children who also have an attention deficit disorder.

To be proactive, talk privately with a learning disabled child early in the year about what the disability is and how it affects his or her reading. You can discuss the specific language-related problems that the child experiences and strategies for overcoming them. It may also be helpful to talk about the many successful people—from entertainers like Cher and Tom Cruise to former governor Nelson Rockefeller and banking executive John Reed—who have learning disabilities.

Conferences such as this should occur on an ongoing basis to provide support and deal with issues that the child does not want discussed in front of classmates. This approach can also prove helpful with other students who are experiencing problems with reading but have not been diagnosed as having a disability.

Working With Students Who Have Attention Deficit Disorders

Debates about Attention Deficit Disorders have become so far-reaching that some experts now disagree about what to call them, as well as what they are and how to treat them. The National Institutes of Health started using the term Attention Deficit/Hyperactivity Disorder to categorize all forms of Attention Deficit Disorders, but A.D.D. remains the commonly used acronym and the one I prefer, as not all children who have Attention Deficit Disorders are hyperactive. In particular, many girls who have A.D.D. do not display signs of hyperactivity and so are not disruptive in the classroom. Instead, they tend to daydream and "tune out," which makes it easy for them to "slide through the cracks" without having their disorder diagnosed.

Attention Deficit Disorders are a neuro-chemical deficiency that interferes with a person's ability to sustain attention, focus on a task, and delay impulsive behavior. Students who have A.D.D. usually show signs of all three characteristics to varying degrees, but a student who does not display all three may still be diagnosed as having A.D.D., whereas another student who does display all three may not be diagnosed as having A.D.D. It's therefore vital to remember that a diagnosis can only be made by a physician or other qualified professional, using an evaluation that usually includes intelligence testing and an assessment of the child's developmental abilities and academic, social, and emotional functioning. A medical evaluation and measures of attention span and impulsivity are also used, along with parent and teaching rating scales. If a child is diagnosed as having an Attention Deficit Disorder, the recommended treatment is usually an appropriate education program, individual and family counseling when needed, parent training in management behavior, and medication when required.

In the classroom, students who have an Attention Deficit Disorder often have trouble getting started on their own and sustaining their work. When given extensive assignments, they may feel overwhelmed and therefore "shut down." Generally, students with A.D.D. respond well to reward-based systems, but these sorts of systems need to be revised often to remain effective. Children with A.D.D. are also likely to need external controls, as they have difficulty structuring themselves, and they need lots of feedback as to how their actions affect others. A very structured, predictable classroom environment, in which rules and expectations are clear and consistent, is extremely important for these students.

In regard to reading, the difficulties created by an Attention Deficit Disorder may also be compounded by a Learning Disability. Many children who have A.D.D. have learning disabilities, and so must receive educational remediation along with treatment for A.D.D. The following recommendations may therefore need to be combined with recommendations from the preceding section.

Reading & Writing Instruction For Students Who Have Attention Deficit Disorders

- Display classroom and reading group rules in one highly visible spot. Make the rules as clear and comprehensive as possible, but keep in mind that having only a few rules makes them easier to understand and obey. Make sure to discuss the rules with students who have A.D.D. and explain the rationale for the rules. Role playing situations involving the rules can also prove helpful, and the rules should be reviewed periodically throughout the year. Your students' parents should also receive a copy of the rules.

- Post a daily reading schedule and write all homework assignments in the same spot every day. Use colored chalk or markers to help A.D.D. students focus on this and other written information. Also tape copies of the daily schedule on the desks of A.D.D. students and others likely to need reminders. In addition, you can tape on index cards that show clock faces set to the time of any sessions with specialists, and write the time of these appointments under the clock faces.

- Before giving verbal instructions, always say the child's name, as this helps the child focus.

- When organizing seating arrangements, remember that you should be in close proximity to your A.D.D. students. You need to be able to make eye contact with them and be near enough to give them visual cues. These students should also be seated near well-focused students who will serve as positive role models, especially during reading group time. Also try to place A.D.D. students in the least distracting part of the classroom.

- Arrange learning partnerships in which a calm or advanced student is paired an A.D.D. child and can help the child learn new concepts or practice previously introduced skills. Peers can also help children who have A.D.D. remain focused on the task at hand.

- Establish a quiet work area where any student can read or do reading-related work. This can be especially helpful for A.D.D. students. You can also make other provisions to help students block out distractions while doing independent reading group work. One possibility is creating an individual "privacy board" but cutting out the bottom and one side of a large, strong, cardboard carton. A child can then decorate it on the outside, which will also provide motivation to take good care of it.

- To carry first graders' homework, give them large envelopes with their names written in large, bold letters. For second and third graders, I recommend having them use a teacher's plan book instead of an assignment pad for homework, because the plan book provides more writing space. When assigning homework, make sure A.D.D. students have their homework notebooks open and are writing the assignment down.

- Train your students to recognize "time-to-begin-work" cues, which may be a hand signal or a special word. Also make the transition between reading activities easier by using attention-getting devices—such as flashing the lights or ringing a bell—to show that an activity is coming to an end and the students must finish what they are doing. In addition, you may want to build in a few brief exercises or stretch breaks between reading activities.

- To increase self-esteem and minimize embarrassment, try to call on A.D.D. students when they are paying attention, and avoid asking questions when they are obviously off-task. Also establish a signal that will remind an A.D.D. child that he or she is off-task. It might be a key word, a hand signal, or a tap on the shoulder. Balance this with positive reinforcement, especially during reading group time, when you can build confidence and self-respect by providing specific praise to A.D.D. students who are doing something well. Rewards such as stickers, prizes, and the right to choose a game to play with a friend can also be very effective.

- Some A.D.D. students find that using a timer helps them attend to their work. Others need occasional time-outs from reading work, which can occur in a part of the classroom that is relatively free of distractions. (However, when time-outs are overused, they lose their effectiveness.) Students who are easily distracted by noise may also need to work in this part of the classroom, and providing them with earphones that block out small noises can help, too. Something else that can help A.D.D. students focus on their reading is having something to fidget with, such as a small eraser or a rubber band.

- Many students with A.D.D. have difficulty staying focused on a page of print and frequently lose their place. Moving a finger or cardboard strip down the page while reading can help. If a child still has difficulty focusing, I make a "tachistoscope" by cutting out a space on an index card, so the child only sees one line of print at a time. A.D.D. students may also lose their train of thought while reading silently, in which case they should be encouraged to use the "reciprocal teaching" technique: Suggest that they think of questions about the material they are reading and have them summarize to themselves what it is about.

• Rather than read silently, some students with A.D.D. need to "sub-vocalize" or read the material quietly to themselves. Hearing their own voices helps them remain focused and aids their reading comprehension. You may need to ask these students to say the words very quietly, but I would recommend allowing them to use this technique, because auditory input is so important to them.

• Much like other types of students, children who have A.D.D. respond better to material that is interesting, relevant, kinesthetic, and multi-sensory. Linking reading material to related activities such as graphing, drawing, and making posters, dioramas, or collages can help them, as can repeated opportunities to verbalize what they are learning. A.D.D. children tend to need help forming images of what they are reading (which good readers do naturally), so you can also suggest that they pretend to be movie directors and make mental pictures of what they are reading.

• When students who have A.D.D. reach third grade and their fingers are long enough, keyboarding can become an extremely helpful skill. If their handwriting is poor and slow, keyboarding can help their hands keep up with and organize their thoughts. See if you can arrange for these students to be taught on a regular basis to use a keyboard. An excellent resource for this is Diana King's *Keyboarding Skills*.

• Where possible, modify work so there is less material on each page, or fold a practice sheet in half so the students can focus on just part of it at one time. These students also benefit from having more time to complete projects, and from having their work organized into lists of tasks that they can check off when completed.

Other Students Who Have Special Needs

You may have other students who do not fit within the parameters of standard special needs categories, but who still have problems that can interfere with the reading process. Following are some additional suggestions for these types of children, who problems are also likely to be alleviated by exposure to appropriate reading experiences.

Late Bloomers - Children who need more time to develop should not be asked to perform tasks they are not yet ready to do. Instead, teach them at their current level, so they learn continually and successfully. Introduce skills slowly and make sure there is ample time for review, all of which encourages late bloomers to persevere. Provide as much exposure as possible to other people reading aloud, whether the reading is done by adults, by peers, or on tape.

Suggest to parents that the family listen to story tapes during car trips. If possible, obtain a copy of *Leo The Late Bloomer*, a wonderful children's book that is especially meaningful for these children.

"Gray Area" Children - Children whose needs are not easily diagnosed and treated—or who do not qualify for a special needs classification for some other reason—need ample review and enrichment. Broaden their experience base and vocabulary by giving them relatively short selections at an appropriate reading level. Choose passages you think would be meaningful to them and preview vocabulary words with them. When possible, take turns reading sentences, paragraphs, or pages with the child, providing a model for correct pronunciation, expression, and phrasing. This can be an enjoyable activity that encourages gray area children to keep reading and that also makes their reading proceed at a faster pace than it would independently or with a peer. Be sure to send notes home praising their work.

Children From Dysfunctional Homes - For these children, books can become a positive, reliable source of support that can prove particularly helpful when the children feel lonely or otherwise needy. So, create a warm, consistent environment and provide materials that are at an appropriate reading level and match their interests and needs. Sometimes, continued resistance to reading on the part of these children may be an emotional issue resulting from problems at home, in which case it should be explored further with other professionals and with the parents.

Children Who Are Socially At-Risk - Books can expose these children to role models they can relate to and learn from, including famous figures who overcame great difficulties, such as Helen Keller, George Washington Carver, and Franklin Roosevelt. Books about sports figures who have inspiring life stories, such as Jackie Robinson, are also likely to prove interesting to many students and have a beneficial effect. There are now many such biographies written at relatively low reading levels, and I have also found that humorous stories and joke books also appeal to these types of children. Try reading these books during reading group time and individually with these students, who also benefit when they can read and laugh together with you.

For these and all your other students, your ability to work effectively with parents and other educators is a vital means of supporting the reading process. The next chapter offers suggestions for implementing a team-based approach.

CHAPTER 7

Developing Your Reading Team

While the classroom teacher has the primary responsibility for teaching a student to read, other adults can and should make important contributions to the reading process. In addition to the vital role played by parents at home, you may also have parent volunteers or aides supporting your reading instruction in the classroom, and specialists and other colleagues working with a range of students on various aspects of reading and language development. Obviously, all of these varied activities can be far more effective when they are part of a concerted team effort, rather than a jumble of disjointed and haphazard events. And, even though a classroom teacher already has more than enough other responsibilities, building and guiding a coordinated reading team can be a great help to students and to the teacher, who is likely to find it enables her to do her job more easily and effectively in the long run.

Knowing that parents should always be leading members of the reading team (and that parents don't always realize this), we'll first explore ways to work with them and then consider other members of the team.

Making Parents Part of Your Reading Team

There are so many valuable aspects of a parent-teacher relationship, you need to make sure parents focus on reading and its importance right from the start of the school year. I recommend sending parents a letter solely about reading early in the fall. In the letter, you can explain that you share their interest in strengthening their children's reading skills and developing their interest in books, and that because they have a vital role to play in the development of their children's reading ability and enthusiasm, you want to provide some initial information and suggestions they can use to help their children.

Knowing that so many parents are themselves enthralled by television, videos, and computers, you need to explain that by reading aloud to their children every day, they are fostering a love of reading and demonstrating how important reading is. And, by reading aloud books that cover subjects of interest to children, but which children cannot yet read themselves, parents are also providing valuable information and supporting their children's interests. Many parents need guidance in choosing appropriate books for their children, so it's helpful to suggest a few books the children would probably enjoy. Also encourage the parents to make regular trips to the local library with their children, and to contact you for names of books that the children can read on their own.

Parents may also need guidance on how to make recreational reading at home a positive experience—as well as an explanation as to why they should do so. Emphasize that reading at a home should be enjoyable, and therefore the child should be able to read almost all the words on a page. I always add that children sometimes just want to browse through a book, and this should be encouraged because it helps them become comfortable and familiar with books. Parents also need to remember that there are many different types of reading materials, and reading suitable sports magazines, video game manuals, and even comic books is worthwhile, because it provides practice and can help children move on to books. Many hobbies, such as cooking and model making, require reading and can therefore also become an important stimulus for practicing reading skills.

After your initial letter, make sure to keep parents apprised of their children's progress in reading. When a child does something special, write or tell the parents about it. Even if you're too busy to write a personalized note, you can use an attractive form. I know both as a professional and as a mother that parents love receiving these messages and children love bringing them home. Some parents have even told me they save these notes and put them in their children's scrapbooks.

Some parents want to do more than "just read" with their children, in which case you can show them how to use their reading time together to develop some important reading skills. Explain that when they take turns reading a book (which should be at their child's reading level), they are helping to develop the child's oral reading—an important reading skill. And, suggest that after reading a book, they always talk about what they have read, as this helps to develop reading comprehension skills. Showing an interest in reading activities at school can also help in this regard, as well as demonstrate the importance the parents place on reading.

Conferring With Parents About Their Children's Reading

Conferences about reading are a key part of your teamwork with parents. Yet, conducting successful parent conferences is an acquired skill and one that requires substantial preparation.

You may therefore want to discuss important points with an experienced colleague or specialist in advance, in addition to assembling and reviewing some of the student's reading-related materials.

To prepare for a conference, I collect the child's phonics notebook, Learning Packet (including some sample reading comprehension work, where appropriate), and the book the child is currently reading during reading group time. After reviewing these materials before the conference, I like to have them available to show parents. I also check the child's reading folder, so I can see samples of previous work, and I review the student's fall reading test, so I can note progress that has occurred in areas covered by the test. In addition, I jot down a few notes about the student's decoding and encoding skills, sight vocabulary, oral reading, and reading comprehension.

Another point to consider is whether any of the child's social behavior seems related to reading. If a child frequently acts out during reading group time, for example, parents should know about this and may have insights about the pattern of behavior, based on comments the child has made to them.

During the conference, I always begin by making a positive comment about the child and describing progress I have observed. I also discuss ways that teamwork between the school and the family can help the child with reading. If this has already started to occur, I make sure to emphasize how it has benefited the child ("It was such a big help when you were able to play the sight word games with Elizabeth. She's finding it easier to recall the words and isn't nearly as anxious about them."). And, I make sure to praise the parents themselves for making the effort. If the parents are not actively assisting their child with reading, you may want to use a hypothetical example or tell about previous students, without mentioning their names.

Also let parents know how important their feedback is, and use an example if possible. I often tell parents about a hard-working third grader I knew, who was learning to write chapter summaries. He did them well at school, but his mother reported that doing them at home had become very frustrating for the child. After further discussion, the child's teacher decided to let the child write rough drafts of the summaries under the teacher's direction and simply copy them over at home.

When sharing information with parents about their child, try to use a matter-of-fact, neutral tone and keep your statements objective. For example, rather than describing a child as "having trouble" functioning in your lowest-level reading group, simply explain what happens during reading group sessions with you, as well as what happens when the child does independent reading work. You should have written observations of specific incidents you can refer to, and be prepared to show dated samples of the child's work, so the parents can see the types of errors being made. This all helps parents understand that you are being informative, rather than judgmental, and it makes them less likely to become defensive or accusatory. It also provides a good starting point for a discussion about what can be done to help the child improve.

Some parents consider their child's reading problems to be a reflection on them and may become rude and hostile even when you present appropriate information in the most positive way possible. Not wanting to be tagged as incompetent parents or even just the parents of a struggling student, they may try to blame you for the child's problems. In this sort of situation, it's important to maintain a professional manner and say what you think parents need to know. In the long run, most parents will respect you for standing your ground. Of course, if you feel a parent is becoming verbally abusive, you should consider asking an administrator to join you or just terminating the conference. And, even if parents remain polite but reject your information and advice, you can recommend that they make an appointment with another member of the staff, whether a reading specialist, guidance counselor, school psychologist, or the principal.

In most cases, however, encouraging parents to talk and "let off steam" about their child's reading can prove helpful for all concerned. Not only does it provide opportunities for you to obtain additional information that may prove valuable, it can build rapport between you and them, which then carries over to the child. Whether children express it or not, they tend to be aware of and influenced by their parents' attitude towards a teacher. With this in mind, I usually suggest that parents tell their child about the conference and recommendations we have discussed, and I ask them to write me a brief note if they get any interesting feedback from the child about what we have discussed. I also suggest that the parents write or call me if they have any further comments or questions after the conference is over.

On occasion, parents may request a conference to discuss their child's reading. In this sort of situation, the parents may be very direct about having a specific matter they want to discuss, or because academic problems can be very difficult to discuss, you may need to give them sufficient time to talk in order for an underlying concern to emerge. One lovely mother came in "just to see how her son is doing." The very active 7-year-old was not yet reading and still having great difficulty with almost every aspect of reading readiness. After we discussed what the child was doing at school and at home, I offered to lend her some of the readiness games her son enjoyed playing at school. Then, as she was getting ready to leave, she asked if I thought her son might be dyslexic or A.D.D. This very private person had needed the rest of the conference to prepare herself to ask what she really wanted to know.

Parents may also request conferences primarily to make sure they are working on a child's reading problems in an appropriate way. They may be more interested in describing what they are doing at home than in hearing about what is happening at school. In this sort of situation, I make sure to praise their efforts and ask about any methods they have found to be especially helpful. And, I try never to let a parent leave conference thinking they did something wrong and I "set them straight." Rather, I try to make them feel that together we brainstormed a problem and devised a new way to handle it.

Working With Parents Of E.S.L. Children

Conferences with the parents of E.S.L. children is an extremely important way to build support for the learning process and work through any misconceptions or other problems, so overcoming any language problems or other obstacles is well worth the effort. If, for example, the parents do not speak English and no adult translator is available through your school, you may be able to have the child or another student serve as a translator.

Parents of E.S.L. students may have strong pre-conceived notions about American schools and little understanding of how our education system actually works. In particular, many E.S.L. parents think of American schools as large and impersonal and have expressed surprise at how warm and supportive their children's schools actually are. I therefore make sure to greet the parents warmly and find ways to show them that I am focused on meeting their child's individual needs. I also mention that I realize how puzzling our educational system can seem, as this helps them overcome any shyness or embarrassment about bringing up questions or issues. And, I find that many parents are delighted when I then offer to explain the system to them.

Generally, the parents of E.S.L. students are anxious to help their children with school work, but if their own English is poor, their ability to provide assistance or even just read stories in English aloud may be limited or even nonexistent. I therefore may suggest that they listen to taped stories with the children, and I recommend tapes that have accompanying story books because, especially in the beginning, looking at the pictures makes the experience more helpful and enjoyable for the children and parents. Some parents may also be able to play the educational games with their children, and when this is possible I show them the games and explain how to play. Usually, the parents are very happy to be able to help their children in this way.

Even when parents' English is so limited that they cannot help with homework, I show them a sample homework assignment and explain what the child is supposed to do, because most parents want to know about this. And, whenever severe language problems may prevent effective communication with the parents, it's important to explain the child's role as a go-between and emphasize your desire to stay informed about things they think are important, as well as answer questions they may have. However, especially with the parents of E.S.L. students, it's important to remember how strongly the parents' background and attitudes may influence how they feel about working with their children in this and other ways.

Working With Parents Of Dyslexic Students

Dyslexic students usually need additional assistance and support in regard to reading, so establishing an effective working relationship with their parents is extremely important. Conferences are a key element of this sort of teamwork, and I usually request that both parents attend if at all possible, because both of them should have an opportunity to ask specific questions about their child's reading difficulties, which they may feel uncomfortable discussing at a general parent meeting. They both may also need an opportunity to express their anxiety or vent their frustration about their child's reading difficulties.

In most cases, it helps to arrange an early meeting with the parents and invite any specialists who are also working with the child. When you all confer together right at the start of the school year, it establishes a basis for working together as a team throughout the year. However, if a child has just been diagnosed as dyslexic and your school has a reading specialist on staff, I would recommend that you have the parents set up a separate appointment with the specialist to discuss the evaluation and diagnosis.

By the end of the first conference, you want the parents to see that you have a carefully thought-out reading program for the child, and that your program is coordinated with the reading specialist's program, so that the programs will reinforce each other and successfully handle the child's problem. To convey this message, start by explaining how your reading program is set up, why it is successful, and how their child will benefit from it. Also discuss the results of your initial reading evaluation and how you will utilize this information.

I always try to emphasize the positive aspects of the child's initial performance in school and mention how much the child deserves the parents' praise and support. I point out how much more difficult getting through the school day is for a child who has dyslexia, and how much the child's self-esteem (and regular discussions about it) can contribute to a successful academic experience. This leads into a discussion about reading books at home, in order to help the child develop an understanding of his or her learning styles and find out about appropriate role models (see the Resource Section for a list of suggested books that can be used for shared reading and for parents to read on their own).

Reviewing other aspects of reading at home is also especially important with the parents of dyslexic students. I suggest that the children read for twenty to thirty minutes each night, and I emphasize the reading should be a pleasure for the children, so they should know about 95% of the words on a page. Often, I find that the parents want and need advice on choosing books that are appropriate for the child's reading level. I also explain how reading at home can be used to support the child's current interests and develop new ones.

A discussion about other types of homework should also be part of the initial meeting. I always ask how long the child spends doing homework, and if the reading is taking too long, I suggest that the parents take turns reading the assignment with the child. If the written part of an assignment is too time-consuming, we discuss cutting the length or modifying the assignment by having the child dictate part of the work to a parent. And, I request that the parents keep me informed about the amount of time being spent on homework throughout the year.

After the initial meeting, make sure to communicate regularly with the parents. Keeping them up-to-date about their child's work is vital, so I frequently send short notes home reporting on their progress or on something especially commendable, which can be quite a pleasant change from the sort of reports the parents have received from teachers in the past. And, don't forget that parents of children who have dyslexia also need reassurance that they themselves are doing a good job dealing with their children's language difficulties.

Finally, I would recommend including a brief, personalized note with a child's first report card, providing additional information and inviting the parents in to discuss the report card further. Obviously, report cards can cause great anxiety for the parents of dyslexic students, so a personal touch can allay concerns and strengthen your relationship with the parents.

Working With Parents Of Children Who Have Attention Deficit Disorders

Virtually all the suggestions in the preceding section of this chapter can also be adapted for the parents of children who have A.D.D., especially because so many A.D.D. children also have learning disabilities such as dyslexia. In addition, you should ask if they are familiar with the organization called Children with Attention Deficit Disorders (C.H.A.D.D.), which provides literature and support groups for parents.

When meeting with parents of children who have A.D.D., I emphasize how important consistency can be. I recommend that a family have only a few rules in regard to school work but make sure they are firmly enforced. I also talk about the value of using reward systems, including one for reading homework. And, I discuss the importance of creating an environment that supports sustained concentration and effort. The parents of one very active 8-year-old told me the child's room contained two stereo systems, one television, a multitude of computer games, as well as a desk lamp which had a revolving, multi-colored base. While they were not prepared to remove all these potential distractions, they did agree to prohibit their recreational use until the child's homework was completed.

Parents of A.D.D. children need to understand homework procedures and goals, as well as the importance of breaking up assignments into shorter segments and including breaks for stretching. As with dyslexic children, I ask the parents of A.D.D. children to contact me if homework assignments appear to be too time-consuming or frustrating, and I promise to let them know right away if I detect problems with the child's completion of homework assignments or other important school work.

Remember that parents of A.D.D. children are often quite anxious about their children's performance in school, so your reassurance and extra efforts are likely to be very much appreciated.

Making Specialists Part Of Your Reading Team

You and your students may be working with a number of different specialists throughout the year. In addition to reading specialists, there may also be speech and language specialists, Title I teachers, resource room teachers, or instructional support specialists helping your students with their reading. This is a lot to handle for everyone involved, so your ability to communicate effectively with the specialists and coordinate your instructional strategies will do much to determine whether and how your students benefit from the different types of intervention.

To establish a team-based approach, open the lines of communication with the specialists right at the start of the school year and let them know that you want to work with them. Explain your expectations and specific needs, and discuss how you can both help each other with students from your class. For example, you can talk about ways to reinforce the work she is doing with your students, and ask for suggestions about your work with specific students, as well as reading materials that would be appropriate for them.

Essentially, you want your students to know that you are working and communicating effectively with any specialists. This would include coordinating about special situations in which the child's best interests should take precedence over standard procedures.

In the classroom, it's important to establish your own authority but also try to be accommodating. You'll probably want to arrange beforehand procedures for having students leave the class for a pull-out session, or where a specialist will work with students in your classroom. (Overall, I prefer pull-out sessions, because working separately with students in the same classroom can be distracting, and it can create anxiety on the part of students who don't want to be seen struggling with material. Pull-out sessions also provide a better opportunity to establish a separate, special relationship with a student.)

Knowing that you both have busy schedules, I would recommend establishing a regular time when you can both discuss your work with specific students. As a reading specialist, I find meetings with classroom teachers very helpful, especially because I can learn how my students' reading problems appear in the classroom. Often, I find that my students need more review time before they can master the reading, writing, and spelling skills that are taught in the classroom, so the classroom teacher and I discuss ways to solve this problem. This could include my spending time on review during my sessions with a student, the classroom teacher modifying her instruction, or a combination of the two.

When we talk about appropriate reading materials for students, we often end up lending each other books and then make sure to tell the students where the books came from, so the students understand we are working together as a team. These sorts of meetings and their results often leave the classroom teacher and myself feeling a renewed sense of energy. And, in between meetings, having an established system for passing notes can also be helpful in this and other ways.

In addition to your work with specialists on the instruction of your students, you may also be called upon to help them and "outside evaluators" with their assessment of a student. Your contact with them may be very limited, but their work can prove very important for the student and yourself, so you need to be well-prepared and keep the following points in mind:

- Especially when communicating with evaluators from outside the school, make sure you have the parents' written permission to provide information about their child.

- To prepare for a discussion with an evaluator, spend some time thinking about the child and his or her needs. Review your notes and samples of the child's written work, focusing on areas of strength as well as weakness, so you can provide information about the child's performance on specific dates, as this gives your input more validity.

- If you are not sure exactly what the evaluator is doing, don't be embarrassed to ask about specific procedures and the reasons for them. This information can give you a better understanding of the results and how you may be able to use them when working with the student.

- At the end of the initial meeting or telephone conversation, set up a mutually convenient time to review the results and any recommendations for further work with the student.

In addition to your work with specialists and evaluators, you also need to be able to work with the cultural influences that are now having such a pervasive effect on today's children. The next and last chapter of this book explores this difficult but important issue.

Working With The Media & New Technologies

Like most educators, I bemoan the vast number of hours so many children now spend watching mindless and often disturbing television programs and videos. And, I'm also concerned about the impact of the video and computer games many children spend additional hours playing. At the same time, I recognize that the media and new technologies can also serve as exciting learning tools, as well as a stimulus for further reading.

Knowing that the media and new technologies will remain with us and continue to be attractive to children for a long time to come, I believe we need to be proactive in counteracting their negative effects and in using them to promote reading as much as possible. We also need to recognize that because books compete for children's time and attention with the media and new technologies, we have to actively promote books and reading as enjoyable, informative alternatives.

With this in mind, let's consider some of the benefits and problems of the media and new technologies, and how we can make the best of them in our classrooms. In addition, because part of our job as educators is to communicate with parents about matters that directly affect their children's reading, let's also consider how we can help make parents part of the team in regard to the pervasive influence of the media and new technologies.

Working With Television, Videos & Movies

Here are some key points to consider:

- The countless hours spent in front of televisions, video games, and computer screens has oriented many children to their visual modalities. We must therefore be ready to reinforce our verbal teaching with written information on chalkboards and charts, using color where possible. Graphs can also be helpful and appealing.

- Violence in games and the media has a disturbing impact on many children. Not only can this lead to imitative behavior and a lack of reliance on problem-solving techniques, I have also found that some young children become so involved with violent cartoons that their independent writing assignments often just rehash the cartoon stories. We therefore need to read and discuss books dealing with alternative conflict resolution, and when necessary require students to write stories that have peaceful conclusions.

- We also need to make sure that children understand that TV shows blend fact with fiction and gloss over the real-life consequences of events like fights and car accidents. Young children may also be exposed to movies and other programming that is not suitable for them and is therefore confusing or anxiety-provoking. When appropriate, this can be a topic for discussions and additional reading and writing projects.

- Children who watch commercial television are subjected to a multitude of advertisements that influence their buying habits and their attitudes. Often, students are happy to talk about the ads they have seen, so discussions and writing assignments about ads can be an effective way to develop literacy skills and consumer awareness. Students may also enjoy doing various types of research about popular products.

- Heavy television viewing results in children having less time for independent thinking and decision making. It also results in children having less time for active play and socializing that encourage these important components of the reading process. The end result can be a mental passivity that leaves children ill-prepared for the active thinking needed to read and write successfully. We therefore need to provide time and support for independent thinking and decision making, especially in regard to reading and writing projects.

- Television viewing does not require children to listen *and* comprehend verbal material at the same time, so heavy television viewers may not develop this important skill. We therefore need to read and discuss imaginative stories, providing time to make sure children understand and discuss new words they learn.

- Incorrect language used on children's programs is one of my pet peeves. One popular cartoon character often says, "Gimme that," and far more inappropriate language is also widespread. To counteract this miseducation, we need to read and discuss books that feature well-spoken characters who engage in high-quality dialogue.

- On the positive side, educational television shows can generate interest in science, social studies, and literature. When appropriate, we should be ready to suggest reading and writing projects that tie in with such shows. There are now also television shows and videos based on children's book characters, so the viewing of the shows at home can lead to reading of the books and discussions about similarities and differences between the two.

Communicating With Parents About Television, Videos & Movies

Due to the tremendous impact television and videos are having on our students, I recommend sending home a "television and video letter" to parents early in the school year, and bringing up related matters as needed during conversations throughout the school year. Here are some key points that should be covered in one way or another:

- Parents should be aware of all the points listed in the preceding section, and they should receive suggestions for helping with these issues at home. Parents also need to understand why reading for information and enjoyment is so important to a child's education and overall development.

- Parents should be aware that numerous studies have shown a negative correlation between heavy television viewing and success in school. Especially when children are having problems in school, television and video viewing habits should be part of any discussion about causes and effects.

- Parents should be encouraged to set specific limits on the quantity and quality of children's television and video viewing, and to use a TV schedule each week to plan the week's viewing, perhaps as part of a "TV contract" that can be written and read in the classroom. As much as possible, there should also be regularly scheduled periods of time devoted solely to reading and writing. And, you may want to pass along the following comment by one astute 11-year-old: "Parents are really stupid when they tell their kids that they can watch TV after they finish their homework, because then the kids just rush through their homework without really concentrating, so they can get to the TV."

- Parents may need to be reminded tactfully that the quantity and quality of *their* own television viewing usually has a strong influence on their children. Time spent together in this way should therefore be devoted to watching appropriate, family-oriented shows for an appropriate length of time. Ideally, this would be followed by related discussions and reading, so as to build literacy skills. Parents also need to understand that they should only have the TV on when they are actually watching a program, because many children are not capable of disregarding it when it is supposed be background noise, and it can therefore interfere with reading and writing.

- Parents should explore other interests with children, such as sports or hobbies. These can then become opportunities for joint participation and related discussions and reading. Parents also need to make sure TV watching does not prevent children from spending appropriate amounts of time playing with friends and toys, and receiving positive adult attention. These important activities can also become wonderful topics for discussions and written material.

Working With Video Games

Video games have many of the negative features of television, videos, and movies, but few of the potentially redeeming social values. In particular, many of the games involve violence, some of it quite gory. And, more than a few children find playing video games virtually addictive. When hours are devoted to playing these games and additional hours are spent watching television, children are even more likely to have little time for and interest in reading at home, as well as related activities.

Most of the points made in regard to television, videos, and movies should be adapted where appropriate to video games. Classroom discussions, as well as reading and writing projects, can help children understand and gain a perspective on video games, and the values and types of activities they promote. In some cases, children who are otherwise reluctant readers are willing to spend hours poring over video game manuals and magazines, and if this is a primary area of interest that stimulates interest in and practice with reading, I am inclined to use it for that purpose, along with other required projects that can help provide balance and perspective.

Communicating With Parents About Video Games

Video games are less pervasive than television, videos, and movies, so you may not need to work with all your students' parents on this issue. However, you should be prepared to inquire about the use of video games and provide appropriate information, especially when a child is having problems in school.

One particularly important point is that video games are rated, but the rating on a video game box is very small, so parents may be totally unaware that their child is repeatedly playing an extremely gory game. In addition, the child may actually be surprised by the extent of the violence in a game he or she purchased. One student told me about an ad which showed scenes from a video game but left out the violent scenes in between them. This sort of violence or other unfortunate aspects of a video game may then become a literacy-related issue, if the violence is repeated in the child's writing or discussions.

As with television and videos, some parents may need tactful reminders about the example they are setting when they play violent video games, and why this can have harmful effects on their child. And, they may need to be encouraged to insist on limiting video game play and making sure an appropriate amount of time is spent reading.

Working With Computers

Computers now have a more ambiguous role in the development of children's literacy skills. The educational benefits of working with computers are frequently emphasized as efforts continue to provide computers and even Internet connections to every school. Yet, my colleagues and I continue to find educational software somewhat disappointing, while the use of computers in school and at home further reduces the amount of time many children spend reading books.

Computers can and should serve as aids in the classrooms, but this can lead to bad habits among students, because many computer programs do not require children to rely on their own resources. Instead, children may be able to continue pointing and clicking until they find the right response. And, while children who have short attention spans or need additional drill may prefer the colorful graphics, exciting sounds, and pure novelty of working with a computer, flash cards are obviously much cheaper and can prove just as effective.

I believe the computer is most helpful when you tie it into your own curriculum and even make your own "programs." You or an aide or volunteer can simply key in comprehension questions for a story you are reading aloud or with a reading group. Then, let a few children gather around the computer, with one designated as the scribe. They can discuss possible answers, and then the scribe can enter the answer chosen. The same sort of thing can be done with some stories and questions, and because many children love working on a computer, students may be even more motivated to do the reading and answer the questions.

Some third graders who have become computer enthusiasts may also like to read and discuss computer manuals and magazines in class. As with video game manuals, this can provide needed motivation for reluctant readers, so I would allow it as a choice when appropriate.

Communicating With Parents About Computers

Many parents are delighted whenever their child spends time in front of a computer, because they think computers are so educational. These sorts of parents need to understand that a computer may be providing entertainment rather than education, and that some computer games are promoted as being educational so that parents will buy them, but their educational value is actually quite poor. The choices given to children are often very limited, and this may be done deliberately so that adult intervention will not be needed. Even when computer games or programs are educational, they may be taking time away from reading books and doing other activities that would be far more helpful.

Parents should also be aware that using a computer can be just as habit forming as watching television, so they now need to impose limits on the amount of time children spend with computers, in addition to monitoring how the computers are being used. Of course, parents should consider the example they are setting with their computer use, as well. Some parents may also appreciate a reminder that reading library books can provide a free but very valuable education, as opposed to the cost of computer hardware and software, the electricity needed to run them, and telephone and Internet access charges.

Working effectively with computers does require children to read the text that appears on computer screens and to enter accurate commands, so access to computers can provide motivation to read and write well. However, reading books and writing on paper remain the most effective ways for young children to develop and practice the literacy skills that will enable them to master the computer and accomplish so much else throughout their lives.

RESOURCE SECTION

Professional Books

de Hirsch, Katrina. *Language and the Developing Child.* Baltimore: Orton Dyslexia Society, 1984, Monograph #4.

Fowler, Mary Cahil. *Maybe You Know My Kid: A Parent's Guide to Identifying, Understanding, and Helping Your Child With A.D.H.D.* New York: Birchlane Press, 1990.

Hallowell, Edward M., M.D. and Ratley, John J., M.D. *Driven To Distraction.* New York: Pantheon Books, 1994.

Hampshire, Susan. *Susan's Story.* New York: St. Martin's Press, 1982.

Rawson, Margaret. *The Many Faces of Dyslexia.* Baltimore: The Orton Dyslexia Society, 1988, Monographs.

Rief, Sandra F. *How To Read And Teach A.D.D./A.D.H.D. Children.* West Nyack, New York: The Center For Applied Research In Education, 1993.

Silver, Larry B. *The Misunderstood Child: A guide for parents of children with learning disabilities.* Blue Ridge Summit, Pa. Tab Books, Division of McGraw Hill, 1992.

— *Dr. Larry Silver's Advice to Parents on Attention Deficit Hyperactivity Disorder.* Washington, D.C., American Psychiatric Press, Inc., 1993.

Simpson, Eileen. *Reversals: A Personal Account of Victory over Dyslexia.* Boston: Houghton, Mifflin Co., 1991.

Vail, Priscilla. *About Dyslexia—Unraveling the Myth.* Rosemont, New Jersey: Modern Learning Press, 1990.

Reading Tests And Assessments

Gates-MacGinitie Reading Tests
The Riverside Publishing Company
8420 Bryn Mawr Avenue
Chicago, IL 60631

Gray Oral Reading Tests (GORT-3)
PRO-ED
8700 Shoal Creek Boulevard
Austin, TX 78757-6897

The Peabody Picture Vocabulary Test
American Guidance Service
P.O. Box 99
Circle Pines, MN 55014-1796

The Wide Range Achievement Test 3
Wide Range Inc.
P.O. Box 3410
Wilmington, DE 19804

Other Professional Resources

Children with Attention Deficit Disorders (C.H.A.D.D.)
l859 North Pine Island Road, Suite 185
Plantation, Florida 33322
(305) 587-3700

Learning Disabilities Association
4156 Library Road
Pittsburgh, Pennsylvania 15234
(412) 341-1515

The Orton Dyslexia Society
Chester Building, Suite 382
8600 La Salle Road
Baltimore, Maryland 21286-2044
(410) 296 - 0232

ADD Warehouse
300 N.W. 70th Avenue, Suite 102
Plantation, Florida 33317
(800) 233-9273

Valued Teaching Tools

Anderson, Valerie and Bereiter, Carl. *Catching On*. DeSoto, TX: SRA/McGraw-Hill.

Boning, Richard. *Specific Skills Series*. DeSoto, TX: SRA/McGraw-Hill.

Bowen, Carolyn. *Angling For Words, Study Book*. Novato, CA: Academic Therapy Publications.

Bush, Catharine. *Language Remediation and Expansion, l50 Skill-Building Reference Lists*. Tucson, AZ: Communication Skill Builders.

Dolch Group Word Teaching Game. DeSoto, TX: SRA/McGraw-Hill.

Dolch Popper Words. DeSoto, TX: SRA/McGraw-Hill.

Edlich, Janet Sutton. *Angling For Words (Sentences For Dictation)*. Novato, CA: Academic Therapy Publications.

Einstein, Carol. *Reading For Content*. Cambridge, MA: Educators Publishing Service.

Elwell, Murray, Kucia. *Modern Curriculum Press Phonics A and B*. Parsippany, NJ: Modern Curriculum Press.

Hall, Nancy with Price, Nina. *Explode The Code*. Cambridge, MA: Educators Publishing Service.

King, Diana. *Keyboarding Skills*. Cambridge, MA: Educators Publishing Service.

Lazzari, Andrea and Peters, Patricia. *HELP 1—Handbook of Exercises For Language Processing*. East Moline, IL: Lingui Systems Inc.

— *HELP 2—Handbook of Exercises For Language Processing*. East Moline, IL: Lingui Systems Inc.

Lindamood, Charles and Lindamood, Patricia. *Auditory Discrimination in Depth*. Austin, TX: PRO-ED.

Makar, Barbara. *Primary Phonics*. Cambridge, MA: Educators Publishing Service.

—. *Primary Phonics Storybook*. Cambridge, MA: Educators Publishing Service.

Mangrum, Charles. *Comprehension We Use*. Geneva, IL: Houghton Mifflin Company.

Mongillo et al. *Reading About Science*. St. Louis, MO: Phoenix Learning Resources.

Power Putty, exercise putty. Randolph, NJ: OT ideas, inc.

Raabe, Janis et al. *Phonics Practice Readers*. Parsippany, NJ: Modern Curriculum Press, Inc.

Steck Vaughn Editorial. *Phonics Readers*. Austin, TX: Steck-Vaughn Company.

Thomsen, Susan. *SPARC*. East Moline, IL: Lingui Systems, Inc.

Traub, Nina. *Recipe for Reading*. Cambridge, MA: Educators Publishing Service.

Children's Literature

Of all the outstanding trade books, I've included only my personal favorites. Many of my students have enjoyed them, and I recommend that you use the books that you love, because if you love a book, you'll communicate this love to your students.

First Grade

Books To Read In One Or Two Sessions

These are excellent books to read in the beginning of first grade. They are short but imaginative books that can be enjoyed by the whole class, so they will make your students eager to hear another story and encourage them to learn to read.

> *Flat Stanley* by Jeff Brown
>
> *Amos and Boris* by William Steig
>
> *The Story of Ferdinand* by Munro Leaf
>
> *The Magic Finger* by Roald Dahl

Shorter Chapter Books

When you introduce the first chapter book, try to make it an important event. You may want to bring in some cookies for the class, as well as emphasize how special chapter books are by telling your class that they are now "grown-up" enough to hear a longer book. And after you read the first chapter, tell them they were wonderful listeners. This praise, plus the story itself, will make the children look forward to hearing the next chapter.

> *Freckle Juice* by Judy Blume
>
> *Fantastic Mr. Fox* by Roald Dahl
>
> *Abel's Island* by William Steig

Longer Chapter Books

These wonderful stories are considerably longer than the shorter chapter books, so before you read the first one, explain to your class that the book will take longer to read. Once the children get involved in the story, they will be eager to hear the next chapter. But, before reading other chapters on subsequent days, ask a volunteer what happened during the last reading. And, at the end of each session, be sure to discuss the chapter that was just read.

James and the Giant Peach by Roald Dahl

The Cricket in Times Square by George Selden

The Boxcar Children by Gertrude Warner

Stuart Little by E. B. White

Easier Independent Reading Books

These are entertaining books that children love to read. And, a good experience reading his or her first book encourages the child to read more. For this to happen, you have to be sure that the child is able to read the book, so ask the child to read a page to you. If the child has too much difficulty reading an initial book, he or she may become discouraged, so it is better for the book to be too easy rather than too difficult. Remember, the goal is to develop an enthusiastic reader!

Green Eggs and Ham by Dr. Seuss.

Harry and the Lady Next Door by Gene Zion (part of a series of Harry books).

Morris the Moose (series) by Bernard Wiseman

Danny and the Dinosaur by Syd Hoff

More Advanced Books

There is a wide range of books here. I find that children of this age love to read series books, so I have included a number of them on this list. I highly recommend the Fox books by Edward Marshall for starters, because they are short, imaginative, and very popular.

The Case of the Hungry Stranger by Crosby Bonsall

Aladdin and the Magic Lamp Adapter Deborah Hantzig

Fox and His Friends (series) by Edward Marshall

Henry and Mudge: The First Book (series) by Cynthia Rylant

Commander Toad (series) by Jane Yolen

Second Grade

Books To Read In One Or Two Sessions

These are wonderful books that can be enjoyed by a wide range of students at the beginning of second grade.

The Magic School Bus by Joanna Cole

Dr. De Soto by William Steig

Four on the Shore by Edward Marshall

Amelia Bedelia (series) by Peggy Parish

Shorter Chapter Books

Second graders want to read chapter books and listen to them, too! Be sure to share their enthusiasm and tell them how exciting you think chapter books are. When you read your first chapter book, make it a special event and bring in a treat. And if you remember, tell them about the first chapter book you read.

George's Marvelous Medicine by Roald Dahl

The Chalk Box Kid by Clyde Robert Bulla

Soup by Robert Newton Peck

Deputy Dan and the Bank Robbers by Joseph Rosenbloom

Longer Chapter Books

These are marvelous tales that require a greater attention span. Explain to your class that these chapters are longer than the ones you read before and tell them that you think that they are grown-up enough to be able to listen. When reading chapters on subsequent days, ask a volunteer to tell the class what happened in the previous chapter. And save enough time at the end to discuss what the chapter was about.

The Indian in the Cupboard by Lynn Reid Banks

Matilda by Roald Dahl

My Father's Dragon by Ruth Stiles Gannett

Bunnicula: The Vampire Bunny and His Friend (4 vols.) by James Howe

The Boxcar Children (series) by Gertrude Chandler Warner

Pippi Longstocking by Astrid Lindgren

Easier Independent Reading Books

Many second graders are still working hard to break the reading code, so you need to supply them with appropriate, interesting material on which they can practice their word recognition and word analysis skills. Remember that independent reading should not be an effort, so the student should know about 95% of the words, excluding proper names.

The Pied Piper of Hamelin by Deborah Hautzig

Singing Sam by Robert Clyde Bulla

Hungry, Hungry Sharks by Joanna Cole

The Gingerbread Boy retold by Harriet Liefert

Nate the Great by Marjorie Sharmat

More Advanced Independent Reading Books

Second graders love to read chapter books, so I've included many of these books below. Like first graders, second graders also love series books, but I have found that not all books in the same series are at the same reading level. It's therefore important to preview each book even if you are familiar with other books in the series.

George the Drummer Boy by Nathaniel Benchley

Freckle Juice by Judy Blume

Muggie Maggie by Beverly Cleary

The Beast In Ms. Rooney's Room (Polk Street School Series) by Patricia Reilly Giff

Chocolate Fever by Robert Kimmel-Smith

Elmer and the Dragon by Ruth Stiles

Third Grade

My comments in the second grade section apply to third grade as well, so I will simply list the books here and refer you back to the preceding section for my comments.

Books To Read In One Or Two Sessions

The Stories Julian Tells by Ann Cameron

The Pizza Monster by Marjorie and Mitchell Sharmat

The King Who Rained by Fred Gwynne

Tales for the Perfect Child by Florence Parry Heide

Shorter Chapter Books

Stone Fox by John Reynold Gardiner

The Good, the Bad, and the Goofy by Jon Sciszka

The Drinking Gourd by F.N. Monjo

Longer Chapter Books

The Mouse and the Motorcycle by Beverly Cleary

Harriet the Spy by Louise Fitzhugh

The Lion, the Witch, and the Wardrobe by C. S. Lewis

In the Year of the Boar and Jackie Robinson by Bette Bao Lord

The Cay by Theodore Taylor

Easier Books for Independent Reading

Shoeshine Girl by Clyde Robert Bulla

Henry and the Clubhouse by Beverly Cleary

Chocolate Fever by Robert Kimmel

Knight of the Kitchen Table by Jon Sciszka

Nate the Great by Marjorie Scharmat

Aliens for Breakfast by Jonathan Etra and Stephanie Spinner

More Advanced Books for Independent Reading

The Three Investigators—The Mystery of the Screaming Clock by Robert Arthur

Matilda by Roald Dahl

Half Magic by Edward Eager

Charlotte's Web by E. B. White

The Castle in the Attic by Elizabeth Winthrop

Books To Read With Children
Who Have Special Needs

Cummings, Rhoda and Fisher, Gary. *The School Survival Guide For Kids With LD*. Minepolis, MN: Free Spirit Publishing, 1991.

Ham, Ray. *What's This Thing Called Dyslexia?* Colleyville, TX 1989.

Janover, Caroline. *JOSH: A Boy With Dyslexia*. Burlington, VT: Waterfront Books, 1988.

Kraus, Robert. *Leo The Late Bloomer*. New York: Simon and Schuster, Inc., 1971.

Moss, Deborah. *SHELLY The Hyperactive Turtle*. Rockville, MD: Woodbone Press, 1989.

Quinn, Patricia and Stern, Judith. *Putting On The Breaks*. New York: Magination Press, 1991.

Game Instructions

Let's Go Fishing

Cut fish out of colored paper and write a word of your choice on each fish. Use a stapler to put a staple on the mouth of each fish. Then attach a magnet to a string for the fishing rod. (If you can find a thin wooden rod, you can attach the string and the magnet to it, and this really looks like a proper fishing pole.) Each child takes a turn fishing and sees how many fish he can catch. His turn is up when a fish falls from the magnet. Then the student reads aloud the words written on his or her fish. When all the fish are caught, the children see who has the most fish.

Robert's Treasure

This is an extremely popular card game, but I prefer using all- purpose labels for playing cards, because the labels are smaller. You can buy a large box of them at most stationery stores, or you can also cut a blank 3" by 5" index card in half.

Some students have difficulty holding playing cards, so at the beginning of the year show your class how they can use a shoe box as a card holder by taking a shoe box and putting the cover under the box. Also show the class how they can stick the cards between the edge of the cover and the edge of the shoe box. As children accumulate pairs of words, they can put them in the box.

The object of Robert's Treasure is to get as many "sets" as possible. A "set" is made up of three matching cards, each of which features a word containing a particular sound or example of a rule. There are 16 "sets" in a deck and four blank cards. There is also a special card called "Robert's Treasure". This card counts as a "set" by itself.

The child who acts as the dealer deals five cards to each player and then puts the remaining cards face down in the middle of the table. This deck is called the "Treasure Chest".

All the players sort their cards, and anyone who has two alike puts them together and then tries to get another in order to complete a "set" of three cards. A blank card can be added to two "word" cards to make a set, but players can't ask for a blank card. Of course, once a player has made a "set" using a blank card, the third word card of that particular "set" is worthless, so players have to be aware of what "sets" are placed on the table.

If a player is lucky enough to already have a "set" of three cards, he or she puts it down on the table, face up. The dealer starts the game by asking if anyone has a particular card, but the dealer cannot ask for a card that he or she does not already have. As long as each card player gets requested cards, he or she can keep on asking for more. If no one has a requested card, the child draws a card from the "Treasure Chest" to finished his or her turn, and the next person to the left gets a chance. If the person called upon has a requested card, he or she must give one or both of them. Towards the end of the game, a player may lose all remaining cards, and when this happens, he or she may draw a card from the "Treasure Chest" in order to remain in the game. The child who gets the most "sets" is the winner.

Memory

This is another favorite game! You can use all-purpose labels or 3" by 5" index cards cut in half for playing cards. Make pairs of words and use them as your deck of cards. You can also use this game for vocabulary development by putting a word and its definition on two cards.

The dealer puts the cards down in rows. He or she turns up two cards and, while doing so, must say the words. If the dealer gets a pair, he puts the cards aside and takes another turn. The dealer's turn is up when he or she turns over two cards that are not matching. Going clockwise, the play continues with each child taking a turn. When all the cards are matched, the children count their pairs. The winner is the child with the most pairs.

Climb And Slide

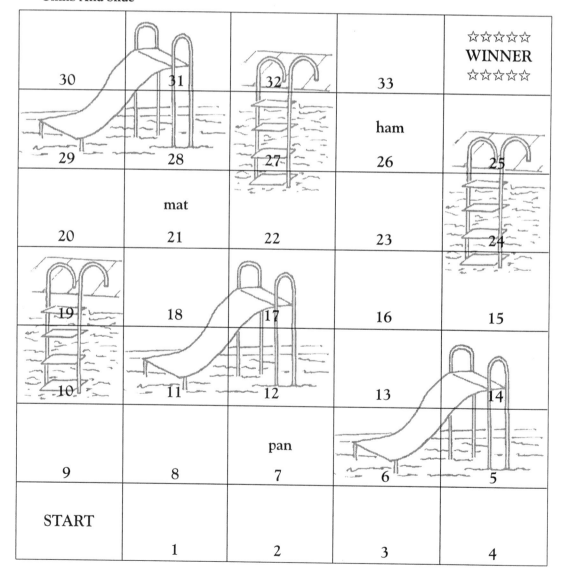

To make your game board (see the illustration above), you can use a piece of colored oak tag paper and cover it with a sheet of acetate paper, or you can use a colored file folder and laminate it. Make the ladders and slides two contrasting colors. Then, using a permanent marker, write the words in the boxes.

When you are teaching a new skill, all you have to do is rub out the old words and write new ones in. You need dice and some game pieces, which could be coins, buttons, or game pieces from an old board game.

The children roll the dice to determine the order of play. The child with the highest number goes first and so on. The player rolls the dice and reads the words as he moves his game piece. The first child to get to the Winner Box wins.

Shoot To The Stars

You can use a piece of oak tag or a file folder for a game board and cover it with a piece of acetate paper or laminate it. Divide the path into units and in each one write a word. Have four or five spaces for special messages like "Star pulls you back three spaces" or "Fuel boost - go ahead three spaces." The game should be played in the same manner as "Climb and Slide."

Indy 500

The object of the game is to see who gets around the track first. Using the same rules as in the earlier games, the children move their pieces around the track. When they land on a Pit Stop space, they must take a Pit Stop Card from the center of the board and read it aloud. When they finish, they put it at the bottom of the pile.

Use a piece of oak tag for the game board and cut out pictures of racing cars from a car magazine to decorate the board. Put a space on the board for Pit Stop cards and use all-purpose labels or index cards cut in half as Pit Stop cards. Make the game more interesting by adding a few surprise spaces such as "Engine Trouble" (go back 3 spaces) etc., and by using toy cars as game pieces.

Bingo

Use large blank index cards or file folders cut in half for Bingo boards. One child is the caller and reads the words from a deck of index cards or all-purpose labels. You can use buttons or pennies for markers. The rules are the same as for the traditional Bingo game.

You can order a sight-word Bingo game called the Dolch Group Word Teaching Game from: SRA/ McGraw-Hill. 220 East Danieldale Rd., DeSoto, Tx. 75115-9960.

Slam Dunk

This is an effective game for reviewing prefixes and suffixes using three-syllable words. Try to use words that are phonetically regular except for the affixes. Use the prefix deck first and when your students are comfortable playing the game, introduce the suffix deck. If you have an aide or an older student volunteer, have that person act as the dealer until one of the students is able to accurately decode most of the words.

Make two decks of cards - 25 pairs of prefix (i.e., *replay*) cards and 25 pairs of suffix (i.e., *wonderful*) cards. Use a bright color to underline the prefix or the suffix. Put 5 Slam Dunk Cards in each set. Here is how you play:

1. The dealer shuffles the cards, puts one card in the middle of the table face up, and says the word.

2. Then the dealer deals one card to each player, starting with the player to the left. As each child gets a card, he or she must read it. Be sure to tell the dealer that if a child needs help, the dealer should help.

3. The dealer continues dealing the cards face up until one child receives a card with the same prefix (or suffix) as the card in the center of the table. The child then says "Slam Dunk". These words stop the play, and the student reads the two words. Once that player has said the two words, he or she can take any other player's cards that have the same prefix (or suffix) by matching the prefixes (or suffixes) and saying the words. When a child gets a pair of words, he or she puts them on the table.

4. Then, saying the word, the dealer puts another card in the center of the table. The dealer continues the play by dealing a card to the next player. The play continues until all the cards are dealt.

5. The children count their cards to see who is the winner. A word card counts as 1 point and a Slam Dunk Card counts as 2 points. The student with the most points is the winner.

Some important points to remember are:

1. When a player receives a Slam Dunk Card, he or she calls "Slam Dunk" and may use the card as a wild card to take the center card. The child reads the word and puts it with the Slam Dunk Card to make another pair. Then the dealer puts another card in the center of the table, and the game continues.

2. If the dealer deals a Slam Dunk Card in the center of the table, another card is dealt on top of it. The child who can take the top card may also take the Slam Dunk Card. He can also take the prefix (or suffix) card of another player by matching the cards and pronouncing the words.

3. When the dealer deals a new card, players having a matching card have to wait their turn to make a pair. When children work well as a group, I let them call Slam Dunk without waiting their turn. It makes the game more exciting. Make clear before the start of the game that if there is a dispute, the dealer has the final say.

Antonym Pairs

This game is an effective way of teaching children the meanings of words. Make a deck of antonym pairs. One child is the dealer and deals 5 cards to each player and the remaining cards are placed face down, in the center of the table. The children arrange their cards, looking for matching pairs (antonyms).

The player to the left of the dealer begins the game by taking a card from the top of the deck. Then, the dealer lays down any pairs in his or her hand. While putting the cards on the table, he or she reads each card, saying, for example, "I have *little* and *big*." Then, the dealer must discard one of his cards and put it beside the deck, face up.

The player to the left has the next turn. This child can take a card from the top of the pack, or take a card or cards from the discard pile (providing he or she has the antonyms in her hand). The game continues until one player has played all of his or her cards, or until the pack is gone and all possible plays are made. The child with the most pairs wins the game.